DISCOVERING COUNTY DURHAM & TEESSIDE

CHARLIE EMETT & RON DODSWORTH

SUTTON PUBLISHING

First published in the United Kingdom in 2007 by
Sutton Publishing Limited · Phoenix Mill
Thrupp · Stroud · Gloucestershire · GL5 2BU

British Library Cataloguing in Publication Data
A catalogue record for this book is available from the British
Library.

ISBN 978-0-7509-4670-4

Typeset in Janson.
Typesetting and origination by
Sutton Publishing Limited.
Printed and bound in England by
J.H. Haynes & Co. Ltd, Sparkford.

CONTENTS

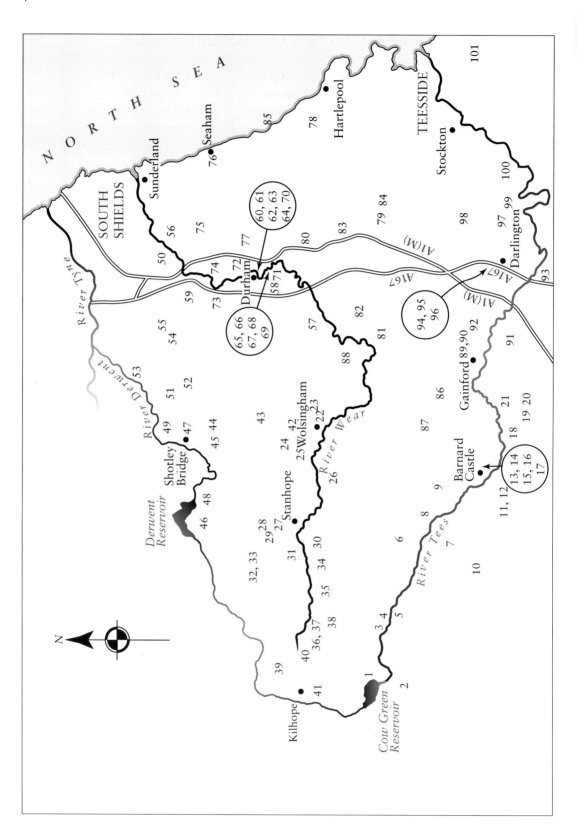

KEY TO MAP OF COUNTY DURHAM AND TEESSIDE

Durham Cathedral (see page 89).

INTRODUCTION

Anyone looking for the very heart of the North-East of England will find that it incorporates all of County Durham and Teesside, a vast area of rich contrasts that is well steeped in history. The whole region is cradled between the High Pennines to the west and the restless North Sea to the east. Together, County Durham and Teesside cover an area of more than 1,000 square miles, most of it essentially rural, between the more populated areas of Newcastle and Gateshead to the north and Billingham and Middlesbrough to the south. Another urban area is centred around Wearmouth, and the rest is rural.

From the Pennines, three major rivers and their tributaries flow eastwards through County Durham and Teesside. The River Derwent, along part of its course, becomes County Durham's northern border. The River Wear has its source on higher ground to the west and follows a tortuous course eastwards before turning north to curl around Durham Cathedral and Castle in a deep gorge. It continues northwards before turning east to follow a more direct route to the North Sea. The Tees is born high in the Pennines, just below the rim of Cross Fell, where the Pennines are at their highest. While still a turbulent mountain stream, the Tees tumbles down Cauldron Snout, a foaming cataract, and then leaps over the dramatic falls of High and Low Force, continuing through a delightful patchwork of pastures, meadows and mixed woodland. All of the Durham dales are in a designated Area of Outstanding Natural Beauty.

As early as 8,000 BC Stone Age man settled between the rivers Tyne and Tees and left his calling cards – flint and stone arrowheads. Then, around 2,000 BC, a new breed of men arrived, who began to clear the forests. This was Bronze Age man, with his bronze weapons. Later still the Brigantes, the largest Celtic group of people in Iron Age Britain, came and took control of all the land between the Tyne and the Humber.

When the Romans arrived the Brigantes fiercely resisted them until AD 43 when they succumbed to the might of Rome. After the departure of the Romans, Angles and Saxons from Denmark and northern Germany settled along the Northumberland coast, and the area between the Tyne and the Tees became wasteland where only wild beasts lived. During the eighth and ninth centuries Christian 'English' became established in places such as Darlington, Wolsingham and Cleatlam, and gradually the pagan Angles and Saxons were converted to Christianity.

It was from these beginnings that Durham developed into a major supplier of coal, which has been mined there since medieval times. In the 1820s the East Durham Coalfield was developed and by 1911 almost 10 per cent of the county's workforce, some 152,000 people, were coal miners. By 1913 England's northern coalfield, 70 per cent of which was in County Durham, produced 58.7 million tons a year, a quarter of the national total. These coalfields have all gone now and the countryside has reverted to its former rural beauty. The 'land of the Prince Bishops' was an ugly duckling that has become a swan. Today County Durham is a delight to explore and, as this book shows, it is a treasure house for those who enjoy hidden places, curiosities, strange events, and warm-hearted people who cherish friendships.

CHAPTER 1

Upper Teesdale

Upper Teesdale.

COW GREEN RESERVOIR

On Widdybank Fell, near the head of Teesdale

1

OS Grid Ref:
810300

Cow Green belongs to one of England's largest nature reserves. It is situated near the head of the River Tees. Some 6,000 years ago Cow Green was covered in pine forest; and today rare Teesdale sedges, characteristic species of pine woods, still grow on the local sugar limestone.

Upper Teesdale is renowned for the uniqueness and richness of its flora, so when it was proposed to build a water reservoir at Cow Green to meet growing industrial and domestic needs on Teesside, the objections, particularly from horrified botanists, were formidable. Nevertheless, Cow Green Reservoir was built, and made a significant change to this part of Upper Teesdale.

The dam was completed in 1970, and in 1972 the first overflow from the reservoir took place. Since then the flow of the Tees has to a large extent been controlled by the reservoir.

Before Cow Green Reservoir was built the indigenous trout were small, and few and far between. Since the reservoir's construction trout numbers have increased sufficiently to make the reservoir a viable sporting fishery.

2

OS Grid Ref:
810283

CAULDRON SNOUT

A short distance south of Cow Green dam

Punctuating the limestone of Upper Teesdale are huge slabs of quartz dolerite, known as the Great Whin Sill, which were formed well below the earth's surface, later to be lifted and exposed to view by movements of the earth's crust. These slabs or 'sills' of quartz dolerite are responsible for the outstanding scenery of Upper Teesdale Nature Reserve, 18,300 acres of upland grazing forming one of the largest nature reserves in England. Here the infant Tees plunges from the rock, creating England's longest and largest cataract, Cauldron Snout, where the river falls 200ft in 200yd, down a series of eight ledges.

Legend has it that a local girl fell in love with a lead miner, but the romance ended suddenly when the miner left her. The distraught girl threw herself into the torrent at Cauldron Snout, killing herself. Today, it is said, her sad spirit can be seen at night on a rocky outcrop alongside Cauldron Snout, singing her plaintive love song.

HIGH FORCE

On the River Tees, 5 miles downstream (east) of
Cauldron Snout

3

OS Grid Ref:
880284

At High Force the River Tees is at its very best. Flowing across a vast area of quartz dolerite, the lively young river gathers pace as it approaches a sudden drop of 70ft into a deep basin at the head of a magnificent gorge. Quartz dolerite is very hard and resistant to erosion, and it forms spectacular cliffs, as seen at High Force waterfall, which is the highest above-ground waterfall in England. The thunder of the water can be heard long before it is seen; and to see it is a must, for no other waterfall has so dramatic and so beautiful a setting. There is nothing graceful about the way the Tees pours over the rock. The fury of its fall is what makes it so memorable a sight.

The northern bank of the gorge below High Force is clothed in deciduous trees, while the southern cliffs are overhung with foliage and topped with juniper bushes.

High Force is the Tees's finest hour.

4

OS Grid Ref:
904280

LOW FORCE

On the River Tees, 1½ miles downstream (east) of High Force

A thick layer of igneous dolerite rock, known locally as whinstone, is what makes the Upper Teesdale National Nature Reserve, of which Low Force is a part, so spectacular. The hardness of this igneous rock gives it a slow rate of weathering and this, combined with the high rainfall of Upper Teesdale, allows acid, peaty humus to accumulate so that heather and bilberry usually dominate the ledges.

Several clusters of Alpine penny-cress have become established at Low Force. They are usually restricted to old lead mine spoil heaps, so to find them growing alongside the River Tees at Low Force is rare.

About 150,000 people visit High and Low Force each year, attracted by their natural beauty and an increasing interest in the scenery and flora. It is to be hoped that the numbers of people visiting Low Force do not spoil what drew them there in the first place.

5

OS Grid Ref:
901279

WYNCH BRIDGE

On the Tees, 1½ miles downstream (east) of High Force waterfall

In 1704 a flimsy bridge was erected across a steep-sided, narrow channel along which the River Tees squeezes. The channel is sited immediately downstream of a spectacular series of low waterfalls called variously Low Falls, Low Force or Salmon Leap. The bridge, said to be the first of its kind in England, was built to enable lead miners to cross the Tees to and from the mines near Holwick village, where they worked. Crossing the shaky structure was hazardous, because it had a handrail on one side only. The bridge was described by a Durham historian, Hutchinson, as 'planked in such a manner that the traveller experiences all the tremulous motion of the chains and sees himself suspended over a roaring gulf on an agitated, restless gangway to which few strangers dare trust themselves'. In 1803 the main chain broke while a group of miners was crossing, and one man was drowned. In 1830 the present suspension bridge was opened to replace the original one.

Today two stone sheep on a nearby wall guard the Wynch Bridge.

RED GROOVES HUSH

On Hardberry Hill, 1 mile north-east of Newbiggin

6

OS Grid Ref:
926291

In the seventeenth century lead mining became an established industry around the head of Teesdale, where rich veins of galena, or lead ore, were to be found along fault lines. A favoured means of exposing the galena was hushing. This involved building an earth dam at the uppermost end of the fault line. When sufficient water had collected, the dam was breached to allow the water to pour along the fault, washing away topsoil and stones, and eventually exposing the galena. These man-made channels ran down the hillsides, or sometimes across them almost horizontally. The great Red Grooves hush, now disused, is very prominent. It appears from a distance as a long gash in the hillside that cuts through a watershed at its midpoint. Although water played an important part in clearing the topsoil and stones from the hushes, preliminary blasting of any rock formation that was in the way had to be carried out. When the blasting and the water had done their work the lead miners took over.

KIRKCARRION

7

OS Grid Ref:
939238

On Crossthwaite Common, a good mile south-south-west of Middleton-in-Teesdale

Kirkcarrion is a conspicuous, circular, walled plantation, wearing a dark green cap of Scots pines, which stands out against the lighter green of the hill on which it is situated. It is found at the eastern end of Crossthwaite Common, on an ancient tumulus or burial mound. It was there that the remains of a Celtic prince, Caryn, were found when the place was excavated in 1804. The name Kirkcarrion is derived from Caryn's Castle. Legend has it that, many years ago, the tumulus was desecrated. Since then, at every full moon, Caryn's ghost can be seen stalking the surrounding hills, seeking revenge for this desecration.

To anyone walking northwards along the Pennine Way, Kirkcarrion is a useful guide. In clear weather it can first be seen at Tan Hill, and thereafter as various ridges are crossed. Kirkcarrion offers brilliant all-round views. From it, Upper Teesdale can be seen in all its spacious glory.

MEMORIAL FOUNTAIN, MIDDLETON-IN-TEESDALE

At the junction of Market Place and Bridge Street

8

OS Grid Ref:
947254

From 1745 onwards the London Lead Mining Company acquired leases of mines throughout Teesdale, and remained dominant until surrendering its leases in the late nineteenth century. Middleton-in-Teesdale became virtually a company town and the London Lead Mining Company brought an element of stability to the area, constantly keeping up to date and ready to spend money on experimentation and developments.

Robert W. Bainbridge was the company's very popular Superintendent, in charge of affairs at Middleton. When he retired in 1877 the employees of the London Lead Mining Company and friends subscribed to a retirement collection for him and Mrs Bainbridge. Having bought them many presents, they found that sufficient cash remained to erect one memorial fountain at Middleton and another at Nent Head. Robert Bainbridge unveiled the Middleton fountain on 28 September 1877. Oddly, this fountain contains four crocodiles, one under each corner of its cover. Why were the crocodiles placed there? Are they playing snap?

ST ROMALD'S CHURCH

9

OS Grid Ref:
995222

On the eastern side of Romaldkirk village

St Romald was probably the son of a Northumberland king. He spent his life in Italy, working with hermit monks. The beautiful church that bears his name is so large that it is known as the 'Cathedral of the Dales'. The original church was Saxon. It was sacked on two occasions, first by marauding Normans and then, in 1070, by Malcolm and his Scottish army. The present church was begun in about 1155 and added to in 1280, with further additions in 1860. It has a walled-up north doorway known as the Devil's Door (see page 140), because it was thought that the devil was living on the north side of it. There is an effigy here of Hugh Fitz Henry, Lord of Bedale, Ravensworth and Cotherstone who, following a distinguished military career, was wounded fighting the Scottish army of Edward I in 1305. He was brought to Barwick-on-Tees, near Darlington, where he died of his wounds on 12 March 1305. He was buried at Romaldkirk, rather than at Jervaulx Abbey where other members of his family are buried, on 22 March 1305.

GOD'S BRIDGE

Just south of the A66 at Pasture End, 2½ miles west of Bowes

10

OS Grid Ref:
956124

From its source on Bowes Moor, the River Greta follows a tightly twisting course along sedimentary bedrock, consisting mainly of calcium carbonate deposited some eight million years ago as the calcareous remains of marine creatures. When the River Greta was being formed a vast slab of this sedimentary rock stretched right across the new bed. There was a weakness in the slab of rock which the river's water found, percolating through it and enlarging it down the centuries, to form what today is a natural bridge, known as God's Bridge.

From the Middle Ages until the coming of the railways God's Bridge was an essential link in County Durham's most important drove road, the Green Trod, which stretched from Cumbria, via Upper Teesdale, to North Yorkshire. On a regular basis cattle, sheep, pigs and geese were taken across it to and from markets. Today God's Bridge is the only natural bridge on the Pennine Way, England's longest footpath.

11

OS Grid Ref:
990135

DOTHEBOYS HALL

*On the south side of the road through Bowes, at the western
end of the village*

Infamous Dotheboys Hall featured prominently in *Nicholas Nickleby*,
the renowned novel by Charles Dickens, published in 1838, which did
so much to expose the monstrous neglect of education in England.
There were then a good many cheap Yorkshire schools in existence,
most of which did not survive the publication of Dickens's book.

It was to Bowes, then a village in North Yorkshire, that Dickens
came in very severe winter conditions while researching the novel;
and in Bowes he found Dotheboys Hall – in reality, William Shaw's
Academy. Dickens based Dotheboys Hall's evil head, Wackford
Squeers, on equally vile William Shaw, using the latter's initials for
the headmaster of Dotheboys Hall.

William Shaw and many of his unfortunate pupils are buried in
nearby St Giles's churchyard. Inside the church is a memorial to one
tragic pupil, George Ashton Taylor, who was only 19 years old when
he died in 1822. This pupil's death so moved Dickens that he used
him as the model for the memorable Smike, whom Nicholas Nickleby
befriended.

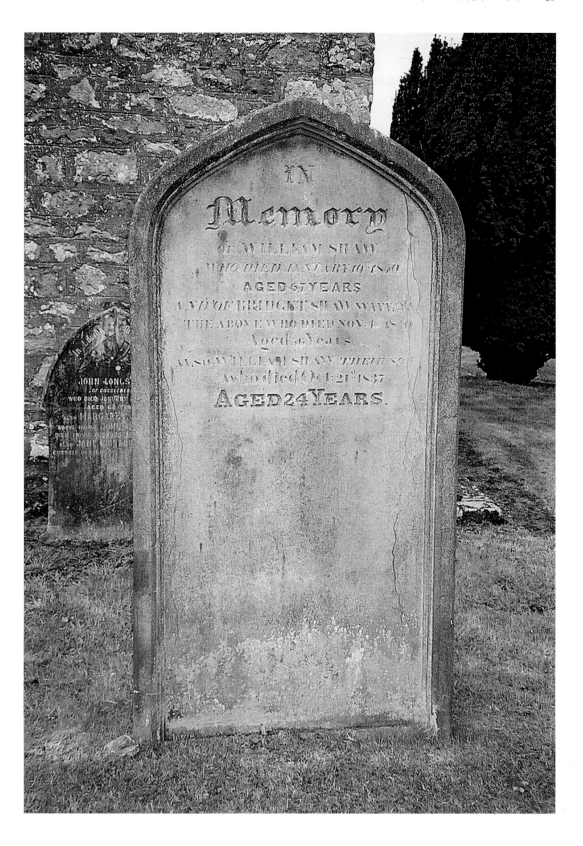

THE ANCIENT UNICORN

12

OS Grid Ref:
996136

On the north side of the road through Bowes, midway through the village

In *Nicholas Nickleby* Charles Dickens described the Ancient Unicorn as the place where the coach carrying schoolboys destined for the notorious Dotheboys Hall stopped. Dickens himself stayed there while researching the book. The Ancient Unicorn was built in the sixteenth century as a coaching inn, and for several hundred years it has been haunted. One owner had a daughter, Martha, who was in love with a local lad called Rodger Wrightson. Martha's parents disapproved of the couple's friendship, so they met secretly on Bowes Moor. One wild night Martha and Rodger arranged to meet, but Martha's father forbade her to leave the inn. Rodger waited in vain,

got wet through, caught pneumonia and died. Heartbroken, Martha lost the will to live and died also. The two were buried in one grave in St Giles's churchyard, Bowes. Years later, the tragedy was immortalised in a poem in which the names were changed to Emma and Edwin. It is Martha's ghost that haunts the Ancient Unicorn today; and the landlady Linda has formed an affinity with this friendly spirit. Her dogs are not so sure. Every time Martha appears their hackles rise.

Recently a couple were seeking overnight accommodation: the husband was shown around the bedrooms while his wife stayed in the car. Everything was satisfactory and the husband went outside to tell his wife that he had booked them a room. She told him to cancel it because the inn was haunted – no amount of persuasion could convince her otherwise.

13

OS Grid Ref:
048163

COUNTY BRIDGE, BARNARD CASTLE

Crossing the River Tees on the west side of the castle at Barnard Castle

Mention is made of a bridge across the River Tees at Barnard Castle as early as 1327, before which time people depended on fords for crossing the river. It is thought that this first bridge was superseded by the present twin-arched Gothic structure, bearing the date 1596. The date is thought to be incorrect: it should be 1569, which is the date when the bridge was repaired, shortly after the Great Northern Rebellion of 1569.

In the eighteenth century there was a chapel on the bridge, where illicit marriages were performed. The services were conducted by a curate called Cuthbert Hilton, who had not taken holy orders but had been trained as a Bible clerk. The bride and groom would be asked to leap over a broomstick while Cuthbert chanted:

> My blessings on your pates
> And your groats in my purse,
> You are never the better
> And I am never the worse.

The chapel is no longer in the middle of the bridge. The bridge itself was severely damaged by the great flood of 1771, but was later rebuilt. Today traffic crossing the bridge is controlled by traffic lights.

BERNARD'S CASTLE

The Castle is on the west side of the town of Barnard Castle, between Market Place and the River Tees

14

OS Grid Ref:
049163

Anyone looking at Bernard's Castle (Barnard Castle), a vast pile, proudly perched on a cliff 80ft above the River Tees, would find it difficult to equate it with the small, palisaded earthwork from which it grew. Yet that is how it all began, as the earthwork was built to guard a ford that carried a Roman road across the Tees. The castle was constructed in 1093 by Guy de Balliol on land given to him by a grateful King William II (William Rufus), in recognition of Guy's loyalty to William I, the Conqueror. When Guy de Balliol died he was succeeded by his son, Bernard, and his nephew, also called Bernard. It was these two men who were responsible for the rebuilding of the castle, which was named after Bernard, the son of Guy. The name was later changed to Barnard. The castle was extended and strengthened several times down the years, and at one time it was owned by Warwick the Kingmaker, from whom it passed to Richard III. It is Richard's emblem, a wild boar, that can be seen on the wall of the Great Chamber.

Barnard Castle is now maintained by English Heritage.

15

OS Grid Ref:
051160

BLAGRAVES HOUSE

Near the north end of The Bank in Barnard Castle, on the eastern side of the road

Innkeeper Binkes Blagraves ensured that he would be remembered by naming his house after himself and then willing it to his eldest son. Seventeenth-century Blagraves House has three mullioned windows, outside steps leading to an eighteenth-century doorway, another doorway to the right of the steps that is thought to be Tudor and a medieval cellar that, until about 1700, was a dungeon. There is a row of ancient-looking carved musicians on a projecting bracket above the first storey, but they are fairly recent, having been placed there in the 1920s.

Oliver Cromwell visited Barnard Castle in 1648 and it is thought that he was entertained at Blagraves House during his stay. When James II came to the throne, local magistrates celebrated the event in Blagraves House.

Joan Forest, whose husband was wardrobe keeper at Barnard Castle for Richard, Duke of Gloucester (later Richard III) for eleven years, until the King's death at Bosworth Field in 1485, displayed his emblem, a bristly boar, at the rear of Blagraves House.

BARNARD CASTLE'S MARKET CROSS

At the south end of Market Place, Barnard Castle

16

OS Grid Ref:
049162

You could be forgiven for not recognising 'Barney's' market cross because it has no resemblance to one. The octagonal structure looks more like a butter market and is generally known as such. It was built in 1747 by a local man, Thomas Breaks, and has served many purposes. At one time all the town's business was conducted here in a large first-floor room and the magistrate's court was held there every month. The enclosure at the centre of the ground floor was once a gaol; and the area surrounding this prison was a butter market where butter, eggs, poultry and other farm produce were sold every market day.

On top of the building's cupola-like belfry there is a gilded weather vane that sports two bullet holes, the result of a shooting match in 1804 between a soldier called Taylor and one of the Earl of Strathmore's gamekeepers. The match was held to settle an argument as to who was the better shot. The two men fired from the Turk's Head in Market Place, about 100yd distant, using the weather vane as a target. If, as is likely, they had one shot each, the bullet holes show that both men were good shots.

Today the market cross – or butter market – is a road island on the A688.

17

OS Grid Ref:
056161

BOWES MUSEUM

On the north side of Westwick Road, towards the east end of Barnard Castle

Designed by the Parisian Jules Pellechet, Bowes Museum was built like a sumptuous French château for Joséphine and John Bowes. Because John Bowes was born illegitimate in 1810, he was not accepted as the Strathmore heir, although he did inherit his father's estates. The rejection caused him to live mostly in Paris, where he owned a theatre. There he met French actress Joséphine Benoîte, whom he married in 1852. Joséphine was a talented painter who shared John's love of the arts. Their passion for collecting artwork grew to such an extent that, at Joséphine's suggestion, they built Bowes Museum to house the expanding collection. Construction began in 1869 but was not completed until 1892, by which time both Joséphine and John had died.

Today Bowes Museum, 100ft high and 300ft long, is one of Europe's finest treasure houses, containing exquisite tapestries, porcelain, furniture, French and Spanish ceramics and paintings by famous artists such as Gainsborough and Rousseau. But the most famous exhibit is an automated, life-size musical silver swan, thought to date from 1773. Joséphine and John bought it for 5,000 francs.

Bowes Museum is in the care of Durham County Council.

EGGLESTONE ABBEY

Just over a mile south-east of Barnard Castle

18

OS Grid Ref:
063151

Egglestone Abbey was founded by Ralph de Multon for the White Canons of the Premonstratensian Order in 1198. It occupies a tranquil setting alongside the River Tees. White Canons were so called because they wore white habits to distinguish them from the Augustinians, who wore black. They chose secluded places for their monasteries, and raised sheep in large numbers.

Egglestone Abbey's peaceful setting did not prevent its being raided by both English and Scottish armies. Consequently, it was always poverty stricken. When it was raided by Scots in 1315 the losses were so severe that the canons' assessment for taxation was halved. In 1328 Edward III pardoned the canons for tax arrears of £16 2s 7d still owed to his father, Edward II. By 1332 the financial situation of Egglestone Abbey was so precarious that Archbishop Melton loaned the canons £20.

In the late fifteenth and early sixteenth centuries the abbey's monks were warned against associating with women of dubious character in the cloisters. By the time Henry VIII dissolved Egglestone Abbey in 1536 the ideal of corporate monastic life had degenerated to a shadow of its former self.

PICKWICK PAPERS CAPERS

19

OS Grid Ref:
008613

South of the River Tees, 3 miles south of Barnard Castle

Was there ever such a setting for a mural? Was there ever such a mural for a setting? Charles Dickens inspired it, and the world-famous Guinness toucan artist, John Gilroy, painted it.

In February 1946, while staying at the Morritt Arms, Gilroy found himself without sufficient funds to settle his bill. So he struck a bargain with mine host in order to clear his debt. Pointing to a ground-floor room overlooking the garden, he said, 'Shut me in there, leave food and drink for me outside the door and do not attempt to enter until I say so.' Gilroy's instructions were carried out to the letter, and on 11 February 1946 he opened the door of the room where he had spent the last few days and invited his host inside.

The full length of the long wall behind the fireplace was completely covered by a magnificent mural of members of the Pickwick Club, gleefully prancing in carefree abandon. A mural on a side wall depicted passengers watching the festivities from the rear window of a stage-coach – and the face of each passenger was a representation of a regular customer at the Morritt Arms!

The proprietor was completely bowled over, and there and then cancelled Gilroy's debt.

The famous mural remains a major attraction and the room, now the intimate Dickens' Bar, also contains several of Gilroy's Guinness paintings. Dickensian evenings at the Morritt Arms, where everything is of the highest quality, are not to be missed.

GRETA BRIDGE

Across the River Greta, 3 miles south-east of Barnard Castle

20

OS Grid Ref:
086132

Elegant Greta Bridge, with its beautiful balustrades, has graced the delightful River Greta since 1773, when it was built by John Sawrey Morritt, Lord of Rokeby, at a cost of £850. Building it was part of a plan by John Sawrey Morritt to improve the Rokeby estate, which he had bought from Sir Thomas Robinson in 1769. The Rokeby estate also included a church, Abbey Bridge over the Tees and magnificent Rokeby House, which was built in the Palladian style, all set in glorious countryside – so splendid Greta Bridge was not out of place.

While researching *Nicholas Nickleby*, Charles Dickens and his illustrator, Hablot K. Browne, stayed at a coaching inn alongside the bridge, which Dickens mentioned in the book:

> The little boys and their united luggage were all put down together at the George and New Inn, Greta Bridge.

In 1805 John Sell Cotman, the famous British painter, spent three weeks at the Rokeby estate, giving Lady Rokeby painting lessons. While there he did a watercolour painting of Greta Bridge, as a result of which the bridge gained renown. The painting is in the British Museum.

MEETING OF THE WATERS

21

OS Grid Ref:
086144

Where the River Greta flows into the River Tees, 3 miles south-east of Barnard Castle

The name 'Meeting of the Waters' inspires romantic imagination and clothes the whole of Rokeby, of which the meeting of the rivers Tees and Greta is part, in vivid colours before it comes into view.

Sir Walter Scott, a great friend of the then owner of Rokeby, found the meeting of the waters and its surroundings so bewitching that, on one visit to the Rokeby estate, he composed much of his famous poem 'Rokeby' in a small cave overlooking the glen through which the River Greta flows to join the Tees. The completed poem carried this dedication: 'To John B.S. Morritt Esq., this poem, the scene of which is laid in this beautiful demesne, is inscribed in token of sincere friendship. G. Walter Scott.' The poem was published in 1813. It helped to make the River Greta a popular tourist destination. J.M.W. Turner's watercolour *Rokeby*, dated 1822, has lines of Walter Scott depicted on two rocks, and other details from the poem are also included.

CHAPTER 2

Upper Weardale

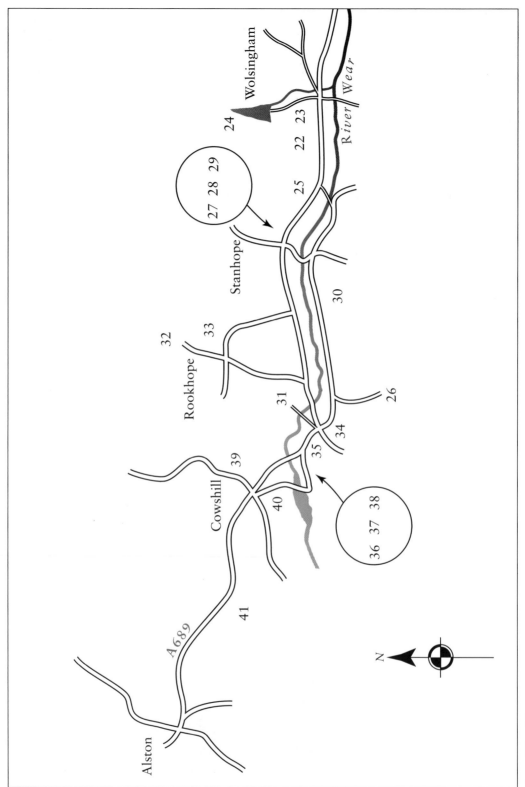

Upper Weardale.

WHITFIELD HOUSE AND PLACE

22

OS Grid Ref: 075371

In the centre of Wolsingham, a Weardale market town

Whitfield House, a three-storey listed building, has stood proudly in Wolsingham High Street for more than 300 years. It was built about 1705, attached to the end of a block of houses called Whitfield Place. It is a splendid structure that adds a touch of class to this Weardale market town. The Whitfields were Northumberland folk and it was Matthew Whitfield of Whitfield Hall, in Northumberland, who had it built. All the windows are oblong and all the rooms are large, some of them panelled. The front door is a double one, made of oak. With such imposing features it comes as no surprise that Whitfield House is commonly referred to as 'the great house'. Yet another feature sets Whitfield House apart from the other houses in Whitfield Place: the evergreens in the front garden. They are holm oaks, which are native to the Mediterranean, and are the only ones in County Durham.

As you stand and face Whitwell House the adjoining house on the left has square windows, while the one on the right has bow windows. Both these houses are dated 1677.

WOLSINGHAM'S HOLY WELL

23

OS Grid Ref:
078379

Close to Holywell Farm on the north edge of Wolsingham

Holy men Godric and Aelric are remembered on the gate of Holy Well. But who are they?

Godric was born in 1069 into a poor Norfolk family. He was first a pedlar, then a seaman, and his travels took him to Holy Island, where he fell under the spell of St Cuthbert and became a pilgrim. Following many adventures he came to Weardale, accompanied by howling wolves, and, exhausted, entered what he thought was an animal's lair. There he was startled to hear a voice in the darkness say, 'You are very welcome, brother Godric,' and was surprised to hear himself reply, 'And may all be well with you, Aelric.'

Aelric was a monk from Durham Cathedral, living as a hermit. He thought that Godric had been sent to see him through his final years. Godric thought that Aelric was his spiritual tutor. Both believed God had brought them together. For almost two years they lived together at Wolsingham, the place of the wolves. Then Aelric died, and was buried at Durham. Some time later St Cuthbert appeared to Godric in a dream and sent him to Jerusalem to prepare himself to go to unknown Finchale. Returning to England, Godric asked some shepherds if they knew of Finchale. They did, and directed him to a cave where he set up a hermitage and lived in it for fifty years, becoming renowned as a sage who wrote songs. The earliest surviving songs in the English language were written by Godric.

That is who the two saints are and why their names grace the Holy Well gate.

TUNSTALL RESERVOIR

3 miles north of Wolsingham

24

OS Grid Ref:
068410

For centuries Waskerley Beck gathered water from the heather-clad millstone grit moors to the north of Wolsingham and carried it southwards into the River Wear. Then the Weardale and Shildon District Water Company, formed in 1866, began building Tunstall reservoir at the head of Waskerley Beck, 3 miles north of Wolsingham. It was built to supply water to places such as Ferryhill, Shildon, Spennymoor and Tudhoe, an area with a population of 112,000. The reservoir, which covers 60 acres, has a capacity of 520 million gallons and is almost 460ft above sea level, was opened in 1880. In 1902 the Weardale and Shildon District Water Company and the Consett Water Company amalgamated, becoming the Weardale and Consett Water Company, which now controls Tunstall reservoir. As the water passes through Tunstall reservoir it is filtered by natural means, becoming very pure indeed.

Set in beautiful surroundings, Tunstall reservoir is home to swans, mallard and trout. The woodland along its eastern shore is full of bird life and carpeted with wild flowers. It is a delightful spot, and the beckside walk from Wolsingham is equally delightful.

FROSTERLEY'S MARBLE FONT

Inside the Church of St Michael and All Angels, Frosterley

A splendid font, fashioned from a piece of Frosterley marble, originally known as 'Forest Lea', now decorates the church of St Michael and All Angels, Frosterley. It had once been used there but had been thrown out because it was considered out of place. It turned up in a church at Gainsborough. Realising that a mistake had been

made in disposing of it, Frosterley's church officials sought to have it returned to Frosterley. But Gainsborough church's groundsman said that although the font had been installed at Gainsborough church in 1888, it had been thrown out and buried in the churchyard in 1967, nobody knew where. Others said that it had been smashed.

After prolonged efforts a pile of stones was found which proved to be the font. They were brought from Gainsborough to Frosterley to be repaired and reassembled. Over a period of 20 years community efforts raised £3,500 for the repair and installation of the font in Frosterley church. There it stands, a proud example of local mineral wealth put to good use.

THIS FROSTERLEY MARBLE AND LIMESTONE, QUARRIED FOR CENTURIES IN THIS PARISH, ADORNS CATHEDRALS AND CHURCHES THROUGHOUT THE WORLD.

26

OS Grid Ref:
018352

BISHOPLEY CRAGS

Alongside Bollihope Beck, 1 mile south-west of Frosterley

Extensive quarrying of 'Mountain Limestone' and mining of galena, or lead ore, was carried out around Frosterley during the Industrial Revolution to provide quicklime for industry and agriculture, and lead. In 1847 the transportation of these commodities was greatly improved by the opening of a railway branch line up Bollihope Valley to the location of several limestone quarries, lead mines and a mill for smelting the lead ore. The single-track line, which connected with the Stockton and Darlington Railway, was routed between Bishopley Crags, a tall, vertical vein of quartz topped with trees, and Bollihope Beck. Where Bishopley Crags squeeze across the route of the railway line to follow Bollihope Beck for a short distance, the railway engineers gave the line a sharp turn away from the beck and through Bishopley Crags, using a narrow gap which they cut through the crags. The gap sides were perpendicular, as tall as the crags and just wide enough for a goods train to pass through – a dramatic engineering achievement.

Close to this man-made cutting, a natural one allows Bollihope Beck passage through the crags. The railway line is no more, but the beauty of Bishopley Crags remains.

THE BONNIE MOOR HEN

Close to St Thomas's Church, Stanhope

27

OS Grid Ref:
991394

The moorhen depicted on the Bonnie Moor Hen inn sign should really be a grouse, because to the miners of Weardale in the early nineteenth century a bonnie moor hen *was* a grouse. The inn was then called the Black Bull.

Locally, trouble had simmered for some time. Miners were not allowed to forage, and several had been caught poaching grouse and been arrested. This infuriated the mining community and a rescue was planned. The rescuers met up with the gamekeepers and the captive miners at the Black Bull and a fierce confrontation developed. The landlord, ill in bed, came downstairs to see what was happening, was attacked by the miners, and fled back to bed. One miner fired a gun up the chimney and then, using the gun as a club, attacked the gamekeepers. The fight was fierce and lengthy, but at last the miners freed their captive friends and the gamekeepers fled. The event lives on in a ballad:

The miners of Weardale are valiant men,
They'll fight till they die for the bonnie moor hen.

28

OS Grid Ref:
991393

STANHOPE PARISH CHURCH

Facing Stanhope market place

At one time the parish of St Thomas, Stanhope was the largest in England and that, combined with the fact that a large number of prosperous Weardale lead mines contributed a tithe of all ore mined, made St Thomas's Church one of the richest in County Durham. So long as the lead mines prospered, a large income was assured for the incumbent. This attractive financial situation resulted in the rector-

ship of Stanhope being held on many occasions by a non-resident bishop. One of these bishops, Joseph Butler, while rector of Stanhope between 1725 and 1740, wrote his renowned *Analogy of Religion*, which is still a major reference source. In it he maintained that the frame of nature showed 'a moral governor revealed through conscience'.

A fossilised tree stump, thought to be 250 million years old, is set into the churchyard wall. It was found in a quarry near Edmundbyers and brought to Stanhope in 1962 by a Mr Beaston. Also in the churchyard are the remains of Stanhope's market cross.

29

OS Grid Ref:
990393

STANHOPE OLD HALL

At the western end of Stanhope on the A689

For hundreds of years an impressive, fortified manor house called Stanhope Old Hall has sprawled across Dilly Hill at Stanhope's western end. People were first recorded residing there in 1135. For centuries the Featherstonhaughs, a powerful Weardale family, made it their seat. They lived there until 1704, when the last male heir was killed in Austria, serving with the Duke of Marlborough. Then, because it was sited near their Upper Weardale hunting park, the Bishops of Durham used it as a hunting lodge. It later became a hotel and is now a very desirable private residence.

Stanhope Old Hall is haunted and is associated with many strange tales. One tells of an engagement party that happened many years ago. The festivities were in full swing when, for no reason, all the lights went out, plunging the merrymakers into total darkness. During this darkness the engaged couple vanished and afterwards couldn't be found. Many years later, while the banqueting hall was being repaired, several floorboards were removed, revealing two human skeletons lying hand in hand.

The present owner, a delightful, level-headed lady, tells of the many ghosts that haunt Stanhope Old Hall today.

HORSLEY HALL

Now Horsley Hall hotel, 1½ miles west-south-west of Stanhope on the minor road to Daddry Shield

30

OS Grid Ref:
966384

For more than 500 years the prominent Weardale family, the Hildyards of Horsley Hall, lived in the great hall and controlled a large estate of tenant farmers. Nearby Westernhopeburn Farm was once one of these tenant farms and the farmhouse is typical of those built in Weardale some 500 years ago. It is a long, stone building of two storeys, with mullioned windows and a stone roof. Most of the front is covered in mellow greenery and its beautiful stone-walled garden is a delightful blend of shrubs, lawns and flowerbeds.

The stone walls and the heavy, stone roof tiles, which blend so well with the surroundings, are a first-class barrier against the roughest weather thrown against them and have a serenity about them that is so often missing these days.

The last of the Hildyards to live in Horsley Hall was E.J.H. Hildyard, a local archaeologist. He wrote a six-volume treatise on Weardale which is a rich source of information about the dale.

31

OS Grid Ref:
953387

ROMAN ALTAR, EASTGATE

Alongside a bus stop on the eastern edge of Eastgate on the A689

The original Roman altar was set up at Eastgate in the third century AD and is now the property of Durham University. The one pictured here, near the bus stop, is a replica. The original altar was found on the east bank of Rookhope Burn, about 300yd north of where the replica now stands.

A Latin inscription states that the altar was set up to Silvanus, the Roman god of the woods and hunting, who was worshipped in all parts of Britain throughout the Roman period, especially by third-century soldiers in a region centred on the hunting country of south-west Durham.

A centurion called Marcus Aurelius Quirinus, whose name appears in the inscription, is known to have been stationed at Lanchester, where he was prefect of cohort Lingonum, an infantry regiment with cavalry attachments, during the reign of Emperor Gordian, AD 238–44. Since region, name and rank all correspond, it is almost a certainty that he was the officer responsible for setting up the altar.

BOLTS LAW WINDING HOUSE

At the top of Bolts Law incline, 1 mile north of Rookhope

32

OS Grid Ref:
940431

The Weardale Iron Company, formed in 1845 to transport iron ore from Weardale, was so successful that it built a mineral line from the sandstone quarries near Westgate to connect with the Weardale and Derwent Junction Railway. The line was 5½ miles long and included Bolts Law incline, which climbed more than 500ft in just over a mile, to reach an altitude of 1,670ft. It was the highest standard-gauge railway in England, and the steepest.

Wagons were hauled up the incline by cables, worked by a huge stationary steam engine sited in a winding house at the top. The line was in continuous use until 1927, after which only horse-drawn wagons used it, carrying supplies for the lead mines around Rook-hope. The line was closed in about 1940 and the tracks were lifted in 1943. Remains of the winding house, locomotive shed and a row of railway cottages remain, a silent reminder of the magnitude of this nineteenth-century feat of railway engineering.

33

OS Grid Ref:
940430

ROOKHOPE INN

In the middle of Rookhope village, close to Rookhope Burn

Rookhope Inn is the only pub in Rookhope, and is unusual because it is run by a committee of local inhabitants. It is Rookhope's principal social centre, the committee is superb, good beer and good conversation flow freely, and the inn thrives.

Here talk is sometimes about the iron and lead ore for which Rookhope was famous, for this village was once an important lead-mining centre with its own smelt mill. Rookhope's first mill was built in 1884, but became 'antiquated' and 'inefficient' so a new mill was built. The new mill had five ore hearths, a slag hearth, a refining hearth and a roasting furnace. The new mill's flue stretched north-westerly, up Redburn Common, where it belched harmful fumes into the fresh air. Today one chimney arch is all that remains of Rookhope's once prosperous lead industry. So, in Rookhope Inn conversation often dwells on locally important matters, such as who put so-and-so in the family way. *Plus ça change; plus c'est la même chose.*

DADDRYSHIELD BURN WATERFALL

A short distance south of Daddry Shield

34

OS Grid Ref:
894374

Daddryshield Burn flows north, through Daddry Shield, to empty into the River Wear, and before reaching this small village it tumbles over a rather nice waterfall. On the west side of Daddry Shield village milkmaids used to milk the cows morning and evening, using the occasion to catch up on the latest gossip. Their meeting place was called 'busy gap', meaning the place where busy people – including milkmaids – gathered for a good 'crack' or gossip. The place where they met was called a 'shieling' or shelter. A man called Daddry lived alongside this pasture and unwittingly gave the village its name, Daddry Shield.

At one time a man called Henderson lived at the village pub. He kept fighting cocks, which he regularly took to Westgate where cockfighting regularly took place opposite the Railway Tavern. Henderson also enjoyed badger baiting, in which these inoffensive creatures were caged and then attacked by dogs. Both cockfighting and badger baiting are now illegal.

Cattle are no longer milked at 'busy gap', but Daddryshield Burn still tumbles over Daddryshield Burn Waterfall, as in days of yore.

35

OS Grid Ref:
887380

ST JOHN'S CHAPEL

1½ miles west of Westgate

St John's Chapel is a market town without a market cross. This was not always the case. At one time a local MP, Ralph Milbank, had a town cross erected as a memorial to the Weardale electors who had returned him to Parliament. The market cross was the only memorial in Weardale and remained so for years. Then in 1866, for no apparent reason, it was demolished and has never been replaced.

The name St John's Chapel is derived from the town's first church, which was dedicated to Jesus our Saviour and John the Baptist. It was granted a licence in 1465 by Bishop Booth. The licence cost £20. The original church was demolished in 1914.

St John's Chapel is the metropolis of Weardale. It was granted a charter, and has a fine town hall where, during the town's lead-mining days, officers met to settle the tithes for lead. For more than a century the Parks and Forest Association has held its annual meetings in the town hall.

The town has had its share of oddballs, such as flamboyant Tommy Dunn who was a leading cockfighting enthusiast. On the day his wife fell into a peat bog on Chapel Fell and died Tommy was at Westgate, cockfighting.

RANCHO DEL RIO

At the eastern end of Ireshope Burn

36

OS Grid Ref:
875385

Originally a school, this magnificent building became the famous Rancho del Rio, the brainchild of a far-sighted couple, Ken and Iris Rowney. Under their skilful direction everything became Country and Western orientated, with mock horse races and lassoing competitions as regular features. Ken's beautiful horse Shandy and a large open fire greatly added to the Wild West atmosphere. Everything was decorated with genuine Native American artefacts, which were continually added to thanks to annual business trips by Ken and Iris to Native American reservations for new purchases. Every aspect of Native American life was displayed and some artefacts, like an elaborate Mexican saddle, were exquisite. They were all displayed against a background of C and W music, and the public loved it.

One dining room was fashioned from canvas, spread to represent the inside of a covered wagon. The tables all faced an end wall showing a view of a Western landscape. The effect was as if dining in a covered wagon; and within this atmosphere countless people lived out their fantasies nightly – and came back for more. The Rancho del Rio was, indeed, a brilliant experience, unique in County Durham and probably throughout the UK.

The place is now an excellent hostelry, the Weardale Inn. The Rancho del Rio lives on in the memories of those of us who were privileged to have shared a slice of Indian life. Ken and Iris Rowney brought magic to Weardale and enriched countless lives.

37

OS Grid Ref:
872325

HIGH HOUSE CHAPEL AND WEARDALE MUSEUM

At the eastern end of Ireshope Burn, next to the Rancho del Rio

High House Chapel is the oldest Methodist chapel in the world and has been continuously in use for services since its foundation in 1760. The Weardale museum occupies the 1804 manse adjoining the chapel, and was formed in 1985.

From its outset, each Sabbath the chapel was filled with people in their Sunday best, singing hymns with great gusto. High House was only the second chapel in Weardale to have an organ. Until the organ was installed in 1883 the singing was unaccompanied.

Joseph Race was probably the best known of the many great preachers from High House. He became the first medical missionary to China, where he died of typhoid in 1880 at the age of 32. His grandson is Steve Race, the well-known pianist and radio and TV personality.

Weardale Museum concentrates on the period from John Wesley's first visit to lead-mining Weardale in the eighteenth century and the subsequent growth of Methodism to the end of Queen Victoria's reign.

JOHN WESLEY'S HAWTHORN TREE

Across the road from High House Chapel, next to Coronation Bridge

John Wesley (1703–91), founder of Methodism, was descended from a long line of gentry and clergy. He was born at Epworth, where his father was rector. He was ordained in 1725 and became a rigid high-churchman. He was appalled at the heathenism of England and took to preaching in the open air. He became convinced that the Christian faith was not a mere acceptance of orthodox opinions, but a habit of soul by which man enters into living union with Christ.

Wesley visited High House Chapel in 1752, the first of thirteen visits over the years, and often preached beside a hawthorn tree outside the chapel because his congregations were so large. He considered Methodism to be a reforming movement within the Church of England, not a different sect. He loved the Anglican Church, and only with great reluctance organised a separate body.

SEDLING MINE

½ mile north-east of Burtree Ford

39

OS Grid Ref:
865409

Sedling Lead Mine was worked by the Beaumont Company from 1818 to 1878 and was a very rich source of lead ore. During its working life the mine produced more than 10,000 tons of lead. The mineshaft was over 400ft deep and the lead vein varied between 3ft and 12ft in thickness.

The Weardale Lead Company became owner of the mine in about 1883, and this company developed two offshoots of the mine that produced more than 17,000 tons of lead ore during the company's ownership. However, between 1900 and 1916 a total of only 3,000 tons of lead ore was produced, as against 50,000 tons of fluorspar, which was extracted near the surface. The lead ore was exhausted in 1948 and Sedling Mine was closed. In 1966 opencast methods were used to extract the fluorspar but extraction operations were ended when the old workings collapsed.

40

OS Grid Ref:
857405

ST THOMAS'S CHURCH, COWSHILL

Overlooking the River Wear at Burtreeford Bridge

Once upon a time Copthill, about ½ mile north of Cowshill, had a church. It also had a quarry, which encroached on the church to such an extent the building became unstable and many graves in the churchyard split open so that exposed skeletons fell into the quarry. The situation became so serious that the church authorities became concerned not only for the remaining graves, but also for the church itself. Following much deliberation it was decided that the church should be moved to Cowshill.

In 1914 the church was dismantled, piece by piece, carted to Cowshill, and rebuilt alongside the River Wear, just below Burtreeford Bridge, where the river plunges over a waterfall. Those graves that had not been damaged beyond repair by the quarrying were also resited alongside the church, St Thomas's. So now all is well and St Thomas can rest easily.

A pub once stood across the road from the church, but it burned down. However, the nearby Cowshill Hotel remains and the beer is good. Between the two buildings, a coach and horse sign graces a road junction and adds a touch of class to this pleasant place.

KILLHOPE LEAD MINING MUSEUM

41

OS Grid Ref: 827428

2 miles north-west of Cowshill along the A689

At Killhope the heyday of nineteenth-century lead mining is recreated exactly where it happened. The mine at Killhope, one of the richest lead mines in Britain, was first worked in 1853 and eventually closed in about 1910. During that period there were many mines in the surrounding moors and dales. The noise of the lead-mining industry would have filled the air, a far cry from today's peace and tranquillity.

The miners were self employed and worked in gangs of up to ten men. They were paid on output and some became rich. But many lived hard and spent their brief lives in poverty. They lived in overcrowded conditions, often sleeping five to a bed. Eating habits were primitive, with people usually sharing a common frying pan. Harmful dust from drying working clothes caused lung diseases and many miners died in their forties.

The giant water wheel at Killhope was built in the 1870s. Then it was just one of many working in the area. Now it is the only one.

CHAPTER 3

Northern Durham

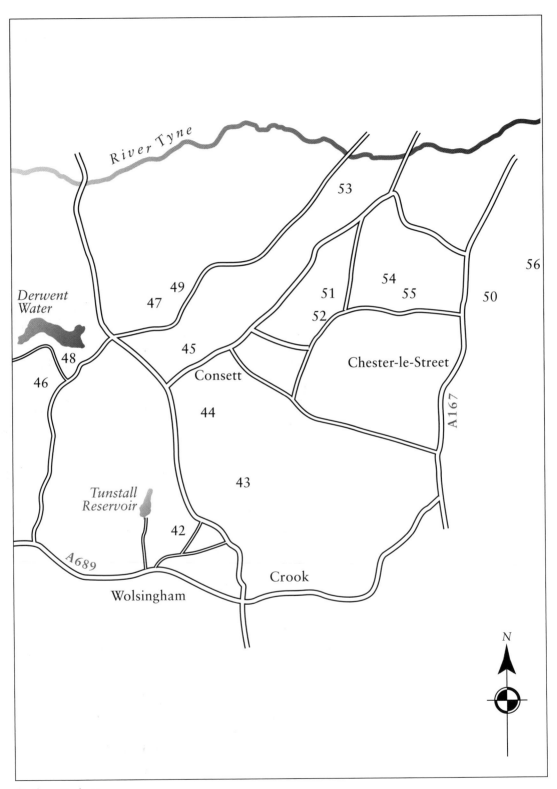

Northern Durham.

REVD JOHN DUCKET, MARTYR

Memorial cross alongside the B6296, 1 mile north-east of Wolsingham

42

OS Grid Ref: 089381

For many English people the year 1644 was a time of uncertainty. Oliver Cromwell was in charge of the country and life for dissenters had become precarious. Many Roman Catholic priests were obliged to carry out their religious duties in secret. One young priest, Revd John Ducket, was returning with two friends to his lodgings in Durham after a christening, when he was arrested by a troop of Cromwell's soldiers. He was in disguise but the soldiers immediately searched him and found holy oils and other accoutrements of his calling secreted about his person. Ducket felt sure he had been betrayed. All three men were taken to Sunderland, where his companions were freed. He was sent to Newgate Prison, London, where he soon learned his fate. He was put on a wicker hurdle and dragged to Tyburn where he was half hanged with a rope. When he was half dead his bowels and heart were removed and his body was split into four parts, taken to Newgate and put on display. Revd John Ducket paid a heavy price for his faith.

43

OS Grid Ref: 117438

STEELEY FARM'S TOMBSTONE

About ¼ mile north of Satey, west of a disused quarry

The tombstone at Steeley Farm is oddly sited, high on the gable end of a field house – and the story behind this is even odder. The tombstone commemorates a farmer of Wharnley Burn who was better known as a highwayman, a reaver and a freebooter. It meant that he could not be buried in consecrated ground, but this did not bother him. He chose a plot on his own land from where he could see

anyone approaching. He continued to live an unethical life and, when it ended, died peacefully in his own bed and was laid to rest in the place he had chosen years earlier. His son erected a tombstone at the grave and successive generations continued to farm Wharnley Burn. Some 150 years later, when the farm changed ownership, the tombstone was removed to its present location at Steeley Farm, but Thomas Raw's remains remained in the original plot until about 1930, when the skeleton was inspected and reinterred. But why was his body left where it had lain for so long? Perhaps the fact that he had been excommunicated had something to do with it.

44

OS Grid Ref:
051452

WASKERLEY

¾ mile south-south-east of Smiddy Shaw Reservoir

From the outset the Stanhope and Tyne Railway had problems. Because of the uneven land it crossed, the line that was begun in 1832 did not open until May 1834, and start-up costs and running expenses caused the company to close in 1840 with debts of £300,000.

In 1845 the Stockton and Darlington Railway, operating as the Weardale and Derwent Junction Railway, took over the line. The same year it was decided to develop Waskerley village as a railway centre. In 1846 a locomotive depot was developed and an engine shed was opened. Offices and stores were built and sidings were laid down. The village was expanded to house the railway workers, and eventually a church, a chapel and a school were built. Because of its bleak moorland location, Waskerley became known for the sturdiness of its railwaymen.

The station dealt with eight trains a day until 1 May 1939, when passenger services ceased. Goods traffic ended on 2 August 1965 and the line was closed on 29 April 1968.

HOWNSGILL VIADUCT

1 mile east of Castleside

45

OS Grid Ref:
097490

The Stanhope and Tyne Railway had a problem. Between Consett and Rowley the line was routed across Hownsgill, a dry valley; but because there was no viaduct the wagons had to be placed onto a cradle, one by one, and lowered on an inclined track to the bottom of the valley, where each wagon was then pushed across the valley floor and onto a similar cradle to be hauled up the other side. This method caused daily bottlenecks. In 1856 the Stockton and Darlington Railway Company sought tenders for a viaduct and chose Thomas Bouch as the engineer in charge of the project. He advised building a slender structure that would allow the wind to blow through. The Hownsgill Viaduct is a superb example of Victorian architecture. Almost three million white bricks were used in its construction. It has twelve arches, each with a 50ft span, and its maximum height above the gorge is 150ft. No one died during the construction of Waskerley viaduct but, sadly, it has become a popular spot for suicides.

46

OS Grid Ref:
046501

MUGGLESWICK GRANGE

Edging Grange Farm farmyard

Muggleswick Grange is on the south side of the River Derwent, which hereabouts marks the Durham–Northumberland border. The thirteenth-century gable, with its two substantial corner towers, was originally part of the Prior's Grange, one of many which the Benedictine Priors of Durham built to accommodate themselves and their entourage when on hunting trips. The estate on which the grange stands is mentioned in the Boldon Book and it had belonged to the priors of Durham before that time. But it was Hugh de Darlington, prior from 1258 to 1272 and from 1286 to 1290, who created a hunting park there and built the grange.

Not far from the grange is Muggleswick church, a small building that is not dedicated to anybody. Nobody bothers about that.

Edward Ward, a local hunter, was a very tall man with big feet. His favourite hound is said to have had a litter of pups in one of his outsize, wooden shoes. Nobody bothered about that, either.

GERMAN SWORD MAKERS

Across the River Derwent from Allensford

It was to Allenford that a colony of German sword cutlers came from Solingen, Germany, seeking religious tolerance. They came during the late seventeenth century and made Allenford the centre of sword making in Britain. They were all gentle Lutherans, and brought with them a secret formula for making the prized, hollow blades. There were several reasons why they decided to settle alongside the River Derwent in the Shotley Bridge area. Shotley Bridge was remote enough from competition; supplies of iron ore for smelting were plentiful; fuel sources were very good; their mills could be powered by the River Derwent; the local spring water was well suited for tempering the steel; and the nearby River Tees was ideal for transporting Gateshead gritstone to the mills. The settlers developed and guarded their skills, and in time a prosperous industry grew up.

Today many locals have German ancestry; the Crossed Swords pub and an inscription in old German on a doorway remain. Translated, the inscription reads:

> The blessing of the Lord makes rich without care, so long as you are industrious in your vocation and do what is required of you. 1691.

48

OS Grid Ref:
015499

THE WITCHES OF EDMONDBYERS

A good ½ mile south of Derwent Reservoir

An 'eye' window in St Edmund's Church, Edmondbyers, is said to ward off ghosts of the many witches believed to have inhabited the area in medieval times. One of them, Margaret Hooper, was reputed in 1641 to have been possessed by the Devil himself. However, the most famous witchcraft trial, held at Newcastle Assizes on 3 April 1673, was when Ann Armstrong and John and Ann Whitfield, all of Edmondbyers, and several others from the surrounding area, were accused of causing death to livestock by changing their shapes and bewitching the wretched animals.

Parts of St Edmund's Church were built before the Norman Conquest. The altar is a single slab of stonework of a type forbidden in the sixteenth century, when it was removed. It was restored to its original position in 1855.

Elizabeth Lee is thought to have been the last witch to live in Edmondbyers. During her life people would carry a crooked sixpence to guard against her spells. She died on 24 January 1792, aged 87. Her headstone can be seen outside the church, on the west wall.

SHOTLEY BRIDGE SPA

49

OS Grid Ref:
091509

At the south end of Shotley Bridge

During the 1840s the popularity of Shotley Bridge Spa was at its height, helped by Dr Augustus Granville, a naval surgeon who, in the late 1830s, having completed a tour of spas in England, found Shotley Bridge Spa 'well situated nearly in the centre of an ornamental garden, about a mile below the village'. He noted that 'the water, which is limpid, and colourless, rises in a horizontal stream, through a spout in an upright stone, which covers the well.' He suggested that it might be instrumental in the recovery of many disorders, which no other water in the country could cure. He added, 'the water differs in its composition from the others I have examined on my recent tour.'

The spa's facilities were developed by a Quaker, Jonathan Richardson, and from 1837 it brought an influx of visitors, including Charles Dickens, who came to Shotley Bridge in 1839. Shotley Bridge developed along Cutlers Road and Snow's Green Road as a direct result of the spa's popularity.

THE LAMBTON WORM

50

OS Grid Ref:
310541

½ mile east of Fatfield

There is a tale told that in 1147 John Lambton of Lambton Hall would spend his Sundays fishing. One day he caught a revolting, worm-like creature which so disgusted him that he threw it back in the water. Down the years the worm grew to a huge size, settled on a rock in the River Wear and terrorised the neighbourhood.

Meanwhile John spent several years on the Second Crusade. On being told about the worm on his return home, he went to see a soothsayer, who said that since he was responsible for its being there, he must kill it. She advised him to wear armour covered with razor-sharp protrusions while fighting it. He also had to make a solemn oath to kill the first living thing that he saw after killing the worm, otherwise a curse would fall on his family.

The battle took place on the mid-river rock. The worm tried to squeeze John, but his sharp bladed armour deeply wounded it and weakened it. John hacked off its head and its body floated away.

Having won, John blew his hunting horn to inform his father. His father, forgetting his son's vow, left the family home and rushed towards the river, where John saw him. Realising his error, John's father returned home for John's favourite dog, which John shot as soon as he saw it. But the shot was too late. His father had been the first living thing John saw after killing the worm and the vow had been broken. The next nine generations of Lambtons all had untimely deaths.

CAUSEY ARCH

From the Causey Arch Inn, left of the A6076 some 2 miles south of Sunniside, cross the A6076 and follow a minor road to a picnic area; walk across it and follow a path signposted to Causey Arch

To reach Causey Arch you descend a man-made embankment that was built in 1725 to carry the Tanfield wagonway, which was powered by horses.

Causey Arch, the oldest surviving railway bridge in the world and for thirty years the largest single-span bridge in Britain, was built by a local stonemason, Ralph Wood, and was completed in 1727. No one had ever built such a bridge before and Ralph relied on Roman technology.

During the late seventeenth century many mine tunnels were being opened and extended, served by the many newly opened shafts in the area. The coal was carried in chaldron wagons that ran on wooden rails and were pulled by horses. As new pits were opened near Tanfield a powerful group of local coal owners called 'the Grand Allies' demanded that a new line be opened to serve these pits. And that was the reason for the building of Causey Arch.

In 1740 an underground fire caused the closure of Tanfield Colliery. By the 1780s the bridge had fallen into disrepair and it became unsafe through lack of use. In 1981 it was restored by Durham County Council.

52

OS Grid Ref:
186555

TANFIELD RAILWAY

Tanfield railway station is 1½ miles north of Stanley

Tanfield Railway was built as a wooden track along which chaldron wagons, drawn by horses, carried coal from the ever more numerous coal pits in the area. The line was a busy one, and during the eighteenth century became one of the largest carriers of coal in Britain. The horse-drawn chaldron wagons were worked with very little rest, the horses reaching the limit of their endurance. Yet 'the Grand Allies' demanded more. By 1841 this unhappy situation was partially resolved by the introduction of steam power. The horses were replaced by stationary engines that pulled the wagons using long cables. The tracks were changed from wood to metal, and before long they became part of the railway system. In 1842 the first passenger service was established on the Tanfield Railway, making it one of the first branch lines to operate in Britain.

In 1881 the introduction of the steam railway locomotive brought to an end 156 years of horse-drawn chaldron wagons and 40 years of stationary steam operation on the Tanfield Railway.

LINTZ GREEN STATION

Half a mile north-west of Lintz Green

53

OS Grid Ref:
150567

At about 10.45 p.m. on Saturday, 7 October 1911 three miners alighted at Lintz Green station from a passenger train from Newcastle. George Wilson, the station master, saw the train off and was walking to his home when he was shot down in an ambush. On hearing the shot the three miners ran back and found Mr Wilson dying in his daughter's arms. The police were called, arrived quickly and searched the area, but no one was found. It is thought that robbery was the motive for the shooting, but no one was ever charged for the crime.

Some 30 years ago, long after the line had closed, a lady who was living at Lintz Green station, now a private dwelling, claimed that on wild, stormy nights she could hear the sound of a train passing through the station.

Two viaducts were built just west of Lintz Green station, and in 1909 a station was built between them. Because it was built of wood, Westwood station was closed in 1942, the first station on the line to suffer this fate, when it became too dilapidated to be repaired.

54

OS Grid Ref:
217546

BEAMISH OPEN AIR MUSEUM

At the north-west corner of Beamish village

Beamish Museum, the brainchild of Frank Atkinson, was opened to the public in 1974. Here, visitors are taken back in time to see industrial, social and domestic aspects of yesteryear, mainly through carefully reconstructed vignettes of eighteenth- and nineteenth-century County Durham. Life in a reconstructed colliery village gives visitors a chance to see how the miners of the area lived and worked in

days gone by. Each building is furnished according to a specific era. Visitors can wander around a town of about 1900 with shops, houses, a stationer's, a sweet shop, a factory, a garage and a working pub. There are guided tours into a real drift mine, a steam engine pulling rolling stock adds to the atmosphere, and a farm concentrates on the life of a yeoman farmer's family of nearly 200 years ago. Original trams, buses and cars transport visitors around the site. Beamish Museum has won many major awards and provided much nostalgia. But if you expect the beer to be sold at 1920 prices, think again.

55

OS Grid Ref:
222535

SHEPHERD AND SHEPHERDESS

The west end of Beamish Village

When the Shepherd and Shepherdess pub was built a couple of statues were placed above the entrance. Each night the figures left their columns and spent the hours of darkness together. He would whisper sweet nothings in her ear and she would whisper sweet nothing-doings in his. Night after night, it was always the same, and as dawn was about to break they returned to their columns. One night the couple became so involved with each other that they lost track of time. At the last moment they decided that they would have to hurry to be on their respective columns before dawn broke. In a panic they sped to their columns and, with no time at all to spare, they made it. Only then did they realise that they had climbed onto the wrong columns – and there they stay. The shepherdess stands on the shepherd's column and the shepherd is on that of the shepherdess. This is obvious to anyone entering the pub, so you can't blame the beer.

PENSHAW MONUMENT

¼ mile north-east of Penshaw Village

56

OS Grid Ref:
334543

Penshaw Monument was erected to commemorate one of the most famous of the Lambton family, John George Lambton, known as 'Radical Jack'. He represented Durham in Parliament and was created the first Earl of Durham in 1833. He became ambassador to Imperial Russia and recommended home rule for Canada. Here, he was ahead of his time, and in the event he was appointed Canada's first Governor General.

Penshaw Monument, a half-size version of the Theseum in Athens, was designed by local architects John and Benjamin Green and was raised by subscriptions from local people following the earl's death in 1840. The work was completed in 1844. The monument has seven columns along each side and four across each end. This fantastic structure never had a roof, but a staircase in one of the huge columns (now closed) gives access to a parapet walkway. Local mine workings blackened the monument and weakened its basic structure. In 1996 the National Trust spent £100,000 on restoration work.

57

OS Grid Ref:
225412

BRANCEPETH CASTLE

Six miles south-west of Durham City

Brancepeth Castle was originally a stronghold owned by the powerful Bulmer family, who developed it into a castle. In 1174 Emma de Bulmer married into the mighty Neville family, who owned the castle until the sixteenth century when, in 1569, it was confiscated by the Crown following the Nevilles' involvement in the Rising of the North and a plot to overthrow Elizabeth I. In 1796 William Russell, a Sunderland banker, bought Brancepeth Castle and the Russells of Brancepeth became one of the four great mining families, known as 'the Grand Allies'. William Russell's son Matthew became the richest commoner in England. When William Russell died in June 1817, followed shortly afterwards by his widow, Matthew moved into Brancepeth Castle and immediately began restoration work, at a cost of over £120,000. The castle's medieval gateway and portcullis, flanked by square towers, were replaced by the huge, Norman-style gatehouse that gives it today's dramatic appeal. Most of the stonework around the central courtyard is no older than about 1826.

NEVILLE'S CROSS

Slightly north of Beaurepaire

Following the Battle of Crécy in August 1346 the English army laid siege to Calais; and Philip of France asked King David II of Scotland to help him by creating a diversion.

At the beginning of October 1346 King David's army invaded England just north of Carlisle and moved along the Tyne Valley, taking Hexham and Corbridge, then crossing the Tyne and heading south.

The English army under Ralph Neville, Henry Percy and the Archbishop of York advanced to Bishop Auckland on 16 October 1346. The night before the two armies met, two monks tried in vain to prevent the Scots fighting, and St Cuthbert is said to have appeared to the Prior of Durham with instructions to carry the saint's banner into battle. The banner was taken to Maiden's Bower, where several monks spent the battle in prayer. The battle was fought on 17 October 1346, and the English army of some 5,000 men soundly defeated the 16,000-strong Scottish army.

After the battle Sir Ralph Neville erected a cross on the site to honour the victory. It was mostly destroyed in the sixteenth century, but part of it can still be seen. Legend has it that if you walk around the cross three times and then put your ear to the ground you can hear the clash of arms.

59

OS Grid Ref:
277512

ST MARY AND ST CUTHBERT'S CHURCH, CHESTER-LE-STREET

¼ mile south of the Civic Centre

In AD 875 the monks of Lindisfarne, threatened by Norse invaders, fled from the island with the coffin of St Cuthbert, and wandered all over the north with their precious burden. In 883 they reached Chester-le-Street, where they built a wooden church in which to put St Cuthbert's body and some other treasures. The body remained there until 996, and during that time Chester-le-Street was the seat of nine Saxon bishops.

During those years many notable benefactors richly endowed St Cuthbert's shrine. King Athelstan was one of the benefactors, bringing all sorts of gifts including tapestries, a cross of gold, chalices and curtains. King Athelstan made a different kind of visit in 937; he

came seeking St Cuthbert's aid during his forthcoming battle with the Scots.

In 995 the threat of Norse invasion again prompted the monks to leave Chester-le-Street with St Cuthbert's body. They went to Ripon, where they stayed for a month until the danger had passed. On their return a new resting place was revealed for St Cuthbert: Dunholm or Durham. Chester-le-Street declined in importance and its church gradually became a ruin.

CHAPTER 4

Central Durham

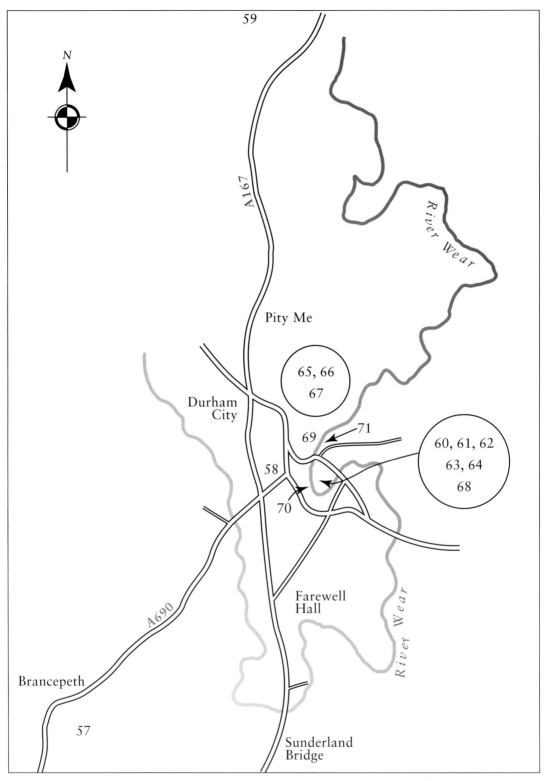

Central Durham.

DURHAM CASTLE

Alongside Durham Cathedral, on Durham Peninsula

60

OS Grid Ref:
273422

Was ever a castle built with so impressive a neighbour as Durham Cathedral? The Lindisfarne monks were the first to erect a fortification on this naturally defensive spot, to protect the shrine of St Cuthbert. The plan worked well and the fort repelled attacks by the armies of both Duncan and Malcolm III of Scotland.

When William the Conqueror broke his journey from Scotland at Durham in 1072, the site of the fort so impressed him that he ordered a castle to be built there. This was done, and it remained uncaptured during the following 400 years of border warfare. Waltheof, the Saxon Earl of Northumberland, undertook the building work and over the years a succession of Prince Bishops added greatly to the castle. In the 1930s a huge rescue operation had to be carried out to underpin the subsiding foundations, for, while the cathedral was built on solid bedrock, the castle was built on less substantial ground.

61

OS Grid Ref:
274422

THE SANCTUARY KNOCKER

Replica set in the north door of Durham Cathedral: original inside the building

During the Middle Ages Durham Cathedral, being a church where the relics of saints, including St Cuthbert, rested, had extra special sanctuary privileges: any hunted criminal would be safe from his pursuers once he had grasped the ring of the sanctuary knocker. The criminal was then given sanctuary and had to wear a simple black gown with a yellow St Cuthbert's cross on the shoulder. This was so that everyone would know that he was a sanctuary seeker. The criminal would have to confess the reason why he was being pursued and this was recorded in a Sanctuary Book. He would then be allowed to stay inside the cathedral for up to thirty-seven days. If by then his pursuers remained persistent or no royal pardon was forthcoming, he would have to leave, bare-headed and wearing his black costume with the yellow St Cuthbert's cross. He would also carry a wooden cross. In theory he had to go directly to the coast and leave the country; in practice he would simply vanish.

DURHAM CATHEDRAL

On Durham peninsula south of Palace Green

62

OS Grid Ref:
275421

When approaching Durham City from any direction Durham Cathedral dominates the landscape. Its setting is magnificent, high on a peninsula formed by a loop in the River Wear. It is heralded as one of the most beautiful religious buildings in the world. On 23 November 1986 the cathedral and neighbouring castle were designated a World Heritage Site by UNESCO. The Norman building looks magnificent, standing perpetual guard over the city. The main church was completed in 1133; its massive stones were quarried locally and brought to the site carved ready for erection. The style of the interior arcading of interlaced arches was probably first used in Durham Cathedral, while the transverse arches supporting the nave vaulting are probably the earliest pointed arches in England.

Inside, the bishop's throne is said to be the highest in Christendom. It was built above the tomb of Bishop Thomas Hatfield, who is reputed to have decided that the Bishop of Durham deserved a throne equal in height to that of the Bishop of Rome – the Pope.

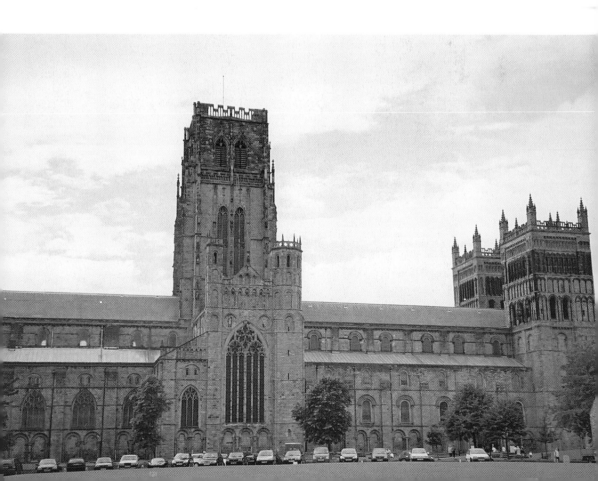

63

OS Grid Ref:
271418

PREBENDS' BRIDGE

Crossing the River Wear at the south end of Durham's peninsula

Prebends' Bridge is a beautiful, three-arched structure designed by George Nicholson in 1777. It replaced a wooden footbridge of 1574 and the stone bridge that replaced that in 1696 and was swept away by a flood in 1771. It was named the Prebends' Bridge because only the prebends or canons of the cathedral had the right to drive a vehicle across it.

From Prebends' Bridge the views of the cathedral are excellent, and it was from the bridge that Turner painted Durham's peninsula – and he knew a good aspect when he saw one. A plaque at the west end of Prebends' Bridge carries an extract from Sir Walter Scott's poem on Durham:

> Grey towers of Durham,
> Yet well I love thy mixed and massive piles,
> Half church of God half castle against the Scot,
> And long to roam these venerable aisles,
> With records stored of deeds long since forgot.

There are two sculptures at the eastern end of the bridge. They are both the work of Colin Wilbourn, former artist-in-residence at Durham Cathedral.

THE POLISH COUNT

64

OS Grid Ref:
272417

Slightly south of Prebends' Bridge on the River Wear

Joseph Boruwlaski was a Polish Count who, because he was only 3ft 3in tall, was referred to as the Polish Dwarf or the Little Count. He was an accomplished violinist and his musical talent brought him many prominent friends and admirers, including Marie Antoinette of France and England's George IV. This remarkable man lived to a great age, dying aged 97, and during his long life he established himself as a respected member of Durham society. He was buried in Durham Cathedral. His grave is marked with a simple 'J.B.'.

The Polish Count lived alongside the River Wear in a diminutive home which, like him, was larger than life. The building that today is still referred to as the Count's House, was, in fact, built during the 1920s in the style of a Greek Doric temple, and is really a folly, built on the site of his home. The Count's House is now neglected, a sad reminder of a little man who was a giant.

65

OS Grid Ref:
274426

ST NICHOLAS' CHURCH

The north side of Durham City market place

The spire of St Nicholas's Church dominates Durham City's market place. But when the original church was built it had no spire, only a small tower. It is thought that the north chancel of the original church was twelfth century and that much of the rest of the structure was medieval.

During its life, the original church was much altered and in 1841 its eastern end was truncated owing to the widening of Claypath at its point of entry into the market place. The building was demolished in about 1855.

The present church, which is almost wholly Victorian, with just a smidgen of Norman, replaced the original one in 1858. It was built to a Gothic design by J.F. Pritchett. When this new place of worship was opened the hymn 'Jesu, lover of my soul', sung to J.B. Dykes's well-known tune, was introduced to a church congregation for the very first time.

THE LONDONDERRY STATUE

In the Market Place, Durham City

The equestrian statue of the 3rd Marquess of Londonderry, in hussar's uniform, was Raffaele Monti's finest work. It was commissioned by Lady Londonderry to commemorate her husband's remarkable life and she wanted to present it to Durham City.

The Marquess of Londonderry's life was one of distinction as an MP both at Westminster and in the old Irish Parliament, and as an army officer. Monti used a new process called copper plating for the statue, and this proved to be expensive. He persuaded Lady Londonderry to pay for the statue in advance, but before the completed work could leave his factory he was declared bankrupt and his creditors seized the statue. Lady Londonderry was forced to pay further large sums. In Durham, businessmen filed a court petition saying that the statue would interfere with access to the market, detract from St Michael's Church and damage business. Fortunately the case was rejected and the erection of the statue went ahead.

Monti claimed that his statue was perfect. Then a blind beggar, feeling the horse's mouth, declared that it had no tongue. Monti was devastated and he committed suicide.

67	
OS Grid Ref: 275425	

NEPTUNE

Formerly sited in Durham Market Place

It seemed like a good idea at the time, if a bit far fetched. By making the River Wear navigable to Durham City, a direct link from there to the North Sea would be forged. The plan to turn Durham City into an inland port was certainly ambitious in the early eighteenth century. So seriously was it considered by many ambitious, influential people with foresight, that a statue was commissioned to commemorate the proposed project.

The statue, by an unknown sculptor, was called Neptune. It was sited in Durham City Market Place in 1729, a symbol of this ambitious plan for the city. The lead figure dominated the Market Place, symbolising the aspirations for Durham City to be joined to the sea.

Unfortunately, the ambitious attempt came to nothing. In 1861 an equestrian statue of the 3rd Marquess of Londonderry was erected in the Market Place. It was sculpted by Raffaele Monti. The statue of Neptune was re-erected in Wharton Park in 1923.

THE BAILEYS AND BOW LANE

Along the eastern side of Durham's peninsula

A bailey is the outermost wall of a castle and the one at Durham is divided into north and south sections.

The South Bailey had its own parish church of St Mary-the-less, now the chapel of St John's College, which was rebuilt in the nineteenth century. The chapel has a sculpture in the chancel, Elizabethan woodwork and a memorial to the Polish Count (see page 91).

There are houses along the North Bailey, some of which are said to be haunted by an elegant lady, some children and a bent man wearing black breeches, an unkempt shirt and a nightcap, seen coming out of a cellar.

In Bow Lane, leading eastwards from the North Bailey, there is an eighteenth-century porch which crosses the pavement. It was to protect ladies alighting from their carriages in wet weather.

Bow Lane leads to the site of the Kingsgate postern, traditionally associated with William the Conqueror. Having tried to open St Cuthbert's coffin to check that the body was incorrupt, he fled on his horse, terrified, and did not stop until he had crossed over the River Tees to the safety of Yorkshire.

<table>
<tr><td>

69

OS Grid Ref:
275425

</td><td>

ELVET BRIDGE: HOUSE OF CORRECTION

Northern arches of Elvet Bridge, Durham City

</td></tr>
</table>

In 1632 a House of Correction was built into the northern arches of Elvet Bridge to house lunatics. It was so used until 1819, when its inmates were transferred to a new gaol at the eastern end of Elvet. The House of Correction remained empty until 1821, when it was sold by auction.

Oddly enough, its most famous inhabitant was not a lunatic, but was a sane gypsy called Jamie Allan from near Rothbury, an accomplished Northumbrian pipes player who was condemned to death for horse stealing. The sentence was commuted to transportation but, because of his advanced age and poor health, he spent the rest of his days in the Elvet Bridge House of Correction. He died there in 1810, the day before the Prince Regent granted him a free pardon. It is alleged that his spirit still wanders the House of Correction and the plaintive sound of his pipes can sometimes be heard.

ST OSWALD'S CHURCH

East of Durham's peninsula in Elvet

70

OS Grid Ref:
276419

Oswald (AD 604–42) was King of Northumbria who, by defeating the Welsh King Cadwallon in 634, had gained supremacy over all the Northumbrian lands. Until then the Welsh king had been ravaging the North. Now, Aidan was able to re-establish Christianity, and at Oswald's request he came with some of his monks from Iona and re-established a monastery on Lindisfarne. Oswald was decapitated by a pagan king, Penda of Mercia, at the Battle of Maserfeith in 642. His severed head was later placed in St Cuthbert's coffin, now in Durham Cathedral.

St Oswald's Church is dedicated to Oswald, who was recognised as a saint. Its west window tells his story. The church's chancel arch and the four eastern bays of the nave date from 1195 and survived the fourteenth-century rebuilding of both the chancel and the north aisle. Mining subsidence caused by Elvet Colliery workings necessitated restoration work in 1834 and again in 1883.

THE ROYAL COUNTY HOTEL

71

OS Grid Ref:
276425

In Old Elvet, Durham City

Old Elvet is, for Durham City, an unusually wide street, once the venue of a horse fair. In 1863 a fountain was placed in the middle of the street, but it was removed before the Second World War. Going westwards along Old Elvet, towards Elvet Bridge, the Royal County Hotel is situated to the right of where the fountain stood.

The Royal County Hotel was formerly two houses, one of which was occupied by Lady Mary Radcliffe, whose half-sister was Lady Mary Tudor, daughter of Charles II. Lady Mary Radcliffe's nephew James was executed after the 1715 rebellion, and his brother Charles is thought to have hidden in Lady Mary's Old Elvet house before his arrest for treason following the 1745 rebellion. Elizabeth Bowes, aunt of Lord Strathmore's wife, Mary Eleanor Bowes, owned the house from 1758.

The Royal County Hotel is famed for its imposing black staircase, which is dated 1660 and was brought to its present site from Loch Leven Castle in Scotland. The hotel's balcony is annually in the news: from here prominent members of the Labour Party acknowledge the Durham Miners' Day parade.

CHAPTER 5

Eastern Durham

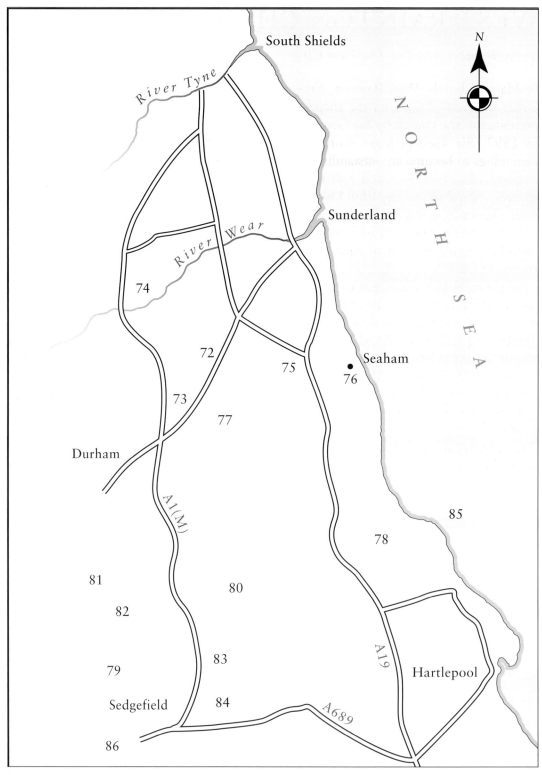

Eastern Durham.

WEST RAINTON CHURCH

72

OS Grid Ref:
323469

4½ miles north-east of Durham City

St Mary's Church, West Rainton, has a strong connection with the Great Pyramid of Giza, in the shape of a memorial tablet that was presented to the church by Sir George Elliot in 1897. Sir George rose from humble beginnings to become an outstanding mining engineer, entrepreneur and politician. He was very proud of coming from Durham and soon after being created a baronet in 1874 he paid for the completion of West Rainton church, the construction of which had been started in 1864.

Sir George's years in Egypt coincided with the opening of its railway and he became much involved with its development. He greatly impressed the Khedive, viceroy of Egypt under Ottoman suzerainty, with his practical solutions to their problems. As a token of thanks, Sir George was allowed to remove some Egyptian antiquities to England.

Sir George also installed a similar tablet in All Saints' Church, Penshaw, where some of his family are buried.

FINCHALE PRIORY

73

OS Grid Ref:
296472

4 miles north of Durham City

The remains of Finchale Priory are partly hidden by foliage on the inside of a bend in the River Wear. It was here that Ethelwald, King of Northumbria, died in AD 765. Church authority at that period was in a parlous state, so the Bishop of Lindisfarne held synods at Finchale Priory in 792, 798 and 810 for the regulation of church discipline.

St Godric, whose story is told on page 38, had strong links with Finchale Priory. After the death of St Aelric, whose disciple he was, Godric built himself a hut in a 'snake infested' area near Finchale. His mother died soon after joining him there and his brother drowned in the River Wear hereabouts; but his sister lived with him for many years. St Godric died on 21 May 1170, apparently aged 105, and was buried in his oratory.

After Godric's death for a while only one monk was living at Finchale Priory; then another monk joined him. In 1241 a church was built at Finchale and it became a holiday home for the monks from Durham.

Today Finchale Priory is probably County Durham's most notable ruined site. It is looked after by English Heritage.

LUMLEY CASTLE

1 mile east of Chester-le-Street

74

OS Grid Ref:
288511

St Mary and St Cuthbert's Church, Chester-le-Street, has attached to it an anchorite's house or anchorage, built to house a hermit or anchorite, who would be walled up inside the structure for a life dedicated to prayer. A narrow slit in a wall of the upper room allowed the hermit to see the altar in the church, while another opening allowed food to be passed to him. The hermit could not see the fourteen stone effigies of the Lumley family, known as 'Lumley's warriors', placed there in 1594 by John, Lord Lumley to honour his ancestors.

Lord Lumley lived in nearby Lumley Castle, which was erected by Ralph Lumley, who was given the land on which to build a fortified house by Richard III and the Bishop of Durham. A multifaceted sundial on a 10ft column stands on the front lawn. Lumley Castle is haunted by the ghost of a white lady, Lily of Lumley.

75

OS Grid Ref:
347505

HOUGHTON-LE-SPRING CEMETERY

6 miles north-east of Durham City, off the A690

One July day in 1856 William Standish was riding along a cliff top when his horse slipped and both horse and rider fell over the cliff edge into a cemetery that had been consecrated just five years earlier.

Standish, who lived at nearby Cocken Hall, was buried close to where his broken body was found, in a vault set into the cliff. Since his death the place has been haunted by a headless horseman, and for years children avoided going near it. But today vandals have taken over. Because of them, the cemetery is no longer used, but on rare occasions the cemetery has an open day. We went to one, following behind a coffin that was carried into the cemetery and placed alongside several others set on raised, wooden supports. We joined many churchgoers gathered in and around a marquee in the middle of the cemetery. There we had refreshments while waiting for the 'Last Post' to be sounded in memory of those killed in the Second World War.

Since Standish did not lose his head in the fall that killed him, why the headless phantom? Blame vandals for that. They broke into the Standish vault, took his head and used it as a football in the cemetery. Not every churchyard is so bizarre.

SEAHAM

76

OS Grid Ref:
435490

6 miles south of Sunderland

In 1820 Sir Ralph Milbanke realised that he could develop his shoreline estate near Seaham to enable coal from Durham collieries to be transported cheaply to London. He asked civil engineer William Chapman to prepare plans for a harbour near Seaham; but before they were completed Lord Charles Henry Stewart saw the plans and realised how advantageous the harbour would be for his new wife's collieries. She was Lady Anne Vane Tempest, who had inherited her father's vast estate, Wynyard Park, and mines at Rainton and Pittington.

Hearing that Sir Ralph was selling his Seaham estate, the Stewarts bought it at auction in 1821 and immediately instructed Chapman to prepare a more ambitious plan. At vast financial expense, a 4-mile-long railway was laid to Lord Stewart's new harbour and construction began in 1828. The first ships were loaded at the harbour in 1830. In July 1881 two sets of loading gear were introduced, allowing Lord Stewart to oversee the loading of coal into his new vessel, the *Lord Seaham*. Lord Stewart had achieved his ambitions: history had been made.

77

OS Grid Ref:
374423

HASWELL ENGINE HOUSE

6 miles east of Durham City

When coal was king, Haswell's contribution to Durham's importance was strong. A pit was sunk in 1831 and the high quality steam coal unearthed ensured that Haswell Plough could develop and prosper. Yet the colliery had flooding problems.

On 28 September 1844 this highly regarded pit, only nine years old, was devastated by a huge gas explosion. A vast cloud of gas enveloped the section of the colliery known as 'the little pit', which was 150 fathoms (900ft) below ground. The blast destroyed the ventilation system, designed to channel fresh air as required. In all, ninety-five men and boys died, fifteen from burns and the others from the suffocating gases produced by the explosion. South Hetton parish church is dedicated to those who perished in the explosion.

When the mine closed in 1895 the sidewall of the winding tower was retained in memory of the fact that it was operated with the first steel rope in the country and, more importantly, as a memorial to those who had perished deep below.

78

OS Grid Ref:
428390

CASTLE EDEN DENE

13 miles south-east of Durham City, off the B1281

The most attractive natural feature of the Durham coastline is probably Castle Eden Dene, an area of magnesium limestone 4 miles long, covering 500 acres. Man has explored the dene for many thousands of years and traces of his occupation, such as flints shaped into tools, have been found there. In 1150, after it had been held by a sucession of owners, Robert de Brus built a 'castle' in the dene. Brus was Lord of the Manor of Eden and built a village, Eden, where Peterlee now stands. It became known as Castle Eden.

In 1758 the successful Burden family from Stockton bought the estate, including the ruinous 'castle', and Rowland Burden senior began building a new residence, which would serve his descendants for nearly 200 years.

In 1850 the Revd John Burden opened the Dene to a fee-paying public and horse-drawn carriages conveyed visitors to the Dene's seaward end, where refreshments were served at Dene Holme. But the twentieth century saw the decline of the Dene's simple pleasures and visitor numbers decreased, as did the Burdens' fortune.

79

OS Grid Ref:
450393

HARDWICK HALL

Near Blackhall Colliery, off the B1261

Hardwick Hall, originally the family seat of John Burdon, stands in parkland landscaped on a grand scale and scattered with follies. The landscaping was expensive and led to the impoverished John Burdon building a house in simple style, quite out of keeping with its setting. In the mid-1750s he created a lake covering 40 acres and creating a riverside scene within view of the hall. In the middle of the lake he placed a statue of Neptune, reached by an elegant, balustraded, single-arched bridge of stone.

Concealed in the roof space of Hardwick Hall there is a priest's hide, a reminder of sixteenth-century religious in-tolerance. A medieval stone gateway lies ruined in a nearby wood, and is surrounded by what remains of a banqueting hall, bathhouse and temple.

Hardwick Hall is now a hotel; but the surrounding parkland, now in the care of Durham County Council, is a public area.

80

OS Grid Ref:
345164

KELLOE CHURCH

5 miles east-north-east of Spennymoor

St Helen's Church, Kelloe, is Norman. It was founded in the thirteenth century as the chantry of the Kellow family, and it was from this church that nearby Kelloe village got its name. Richard Kellow became Prince Bishop of Durham in the thirteenth century.

Inside the church the 700-year-old bells are rung regularly and a beautifully restored coat of arms which belonged to Charles II is on display. There is also an exquisite early twelfth-century cross, which is thought to have been sculpted in France. It was once brilliantly coloured and gilded. It stands against the sanctuary's north wall. There are nine cavities in the cross, which may have held jewels or coloured crystal stones. The cross is regarded as one of the finest Norman sculptures in County Durham.

Elizabeth Barrett Browning's family lived at nearby Coxhoe Hall, now demolished, and she was baptised at St Helen's Church, in the font that is still in use today.

WHITWORTH HALL

4 miles east of Bishop Auckland

81

OS Grid Ref:
236348

Set in 100 acres of deer park, Whitworth Hall was built in 1183 and has had many owners down the years. One, the Earl of Westmorland, lost the estate to the Crown for treason. The hall was completely remodelled in about 1820; then in 1876 it was devastated by fire.
Whitworth Hall's most famous owners were the Shafto family. In the eighteenth century Robert Duncombe Shafto, MP, became famous through the ballad 'Bonny Bobby Shafto', an electioneering song that popularised his financially disastrous courtships. The Shaftos left Whitworth Hall in about 1829.

   The charming rose arbour adorning the hall's garden was given to one of the Shafto family by another prominent Durham family, the Salvins of Burn Hall, as a wedding present.

   The parish churchyard stands in the grounds of Whitworth Hall. There are two thirteenth-century effigies alongside the hall's west wall. One is of a recumbent knight, his feet resting on a human figure. He is thought to be Thomas de Acle, who died in about 1290. The other, of a woman praying, is probably his wife.

82

OS Grid Ref:
263314

KIRK MERRINGTON

3 miles north-east of Bishop Auckland

The day 25 January 1683 was a filthy one. Louis and Margaret Brass were returning home to High Hill House, just outside Ferryhill, anxious to thaw out. The winter wind was chilling, but not, as they would find out, as bitter as the scene awaiting them when they entered their house.

The bodies of their children confronted them: all three had been murdered. Andrew Mills, the Brasses' servant and a simpleton, confessed to the murders and was executed. His body was exhibited at a crossroads north of Ferryhill. The children were buried in nearby Kirk Merrington churchyard and the tombstone's inscription read:

Here lie the bodies of John, Jane and Elizabeth, children of Louis and Margaret Brass murdered on January 25th, 1683 by Andrew Mills . . .

Mills's father did not agree with the verdict and for the next twenty years he repeatedly removed the word 'guilty' from the tombstone. The defaced tombstone was restored in 1757, but the groove is still visible. The epitaph reads:

Reader, remember, sleeping we were slain,
And here we sleep till we must rise again . . .

BISHOP MIDDLEHAM: THE DUN COW

83

7 miles south-east of Durham City

OS Grid Ref:
329305

In AD 995 a group of Christians led by Bishop Ealdhum had been instructed to carry the body of St Cuthbert to a place of safety called Dunholme. But they had a problem. No one had any idea where this place of safety was; none of the group had heard of it. So, where could it be? That was the rub. For them it was a serious problem because it was imperative that the coffin they were so jealously guarding was placed in this secure burial ground.

They were close to Bishop Middleham when their prayers were answered. They heard a milkmaid calling for her lost cow and, more importantly, they heard someone reply. The person told her that she would find her cow at a place called Dunholme. Dunholme! The pilgrims couldn't believe their luck. They followed the milkmaid, who led them to a rocky promontory, which they felt in their bones was the place they were seeking. They buried St Cuthbert and erected a shrine to his memory. From that shrine grew Durham Cathedral and city.

SEDGEFIELD BALL GAME

84

OS Grid Ref:
354287

9 miles east of Bishop Auckland

A very special ball game is played in Sedgefield every Shrove Tuesday, and it is unique. It originated in 1072, probably as a final fling before the fasting of Lent. It began as a contest between artisans and farm workers. A small leather ball, made secretly by a Darlington saddler and supplied by local publicans, was passed through a bull's nose-ring at the northern end of the town's green by a local resident or previous player. Then, when the church clock showed 1 p.m. a starter shouted 'Alley off!' and threw the ball into the throng.

Goals or alleying places are set about ¼ mile apart. The ball is kicked, carried and thrown all around Sedgefield, and for that one day no garden is out of bounds. The ball has to go into every public house before reaching a goal. If the ball has not been alleyed by 6 p.m. it becomes the property of the sexton.

BLACKHALL ROCKS

A short distance south of Blackhall village

It has taken the pounding of countless tides, wearing away at County Durham's coastal cliffs near Blackhall village, to make Blackhall Rocks so attractive to the many visitors drawn to them. Down the centuries coastal erosion has isolated parts of the mainland, attacking the weakest parts of both the mainland mass and the detached pieces, rocky outcrops in the sea. Large, cavernous openings have been gouged out of the cliffs and an outlier has had a huge opening tunnelled through it. It is an ongoing situation, a continual battle waged by the sea on an ever-changing coastline.

Blackhall was the scene of an unusual find in 1916. A stone cist was discovered that contained the body of a child, thought to be Anglo Saxon. Nothing else was in the cist, apart from a bead, probably left there by accident. It is thought, therefore, that this could have been a pagan burial, and judging by the way the body was positioned, it could have been Iron Age or Bronze Age.

86

OS Grid Ref:
238256

SHILDON: TIMOTHY HACKWORTH

1½ miles south-south-east of Bishop Auckland

Timothy Hackworth is possibly the most unsung of the railway pioneers. He was born in Wylam on 22 December 1786, and by 28 June 1825 he was resident engineer at Shildon to the Stockton and Darlington Railway. There he built the *Royal George*, the first locomotive on which cylinders drove the wheels directly. First used in 1827, the locomotive was so successful that it became the forerunner of several heavier engines. In 1837 he built the first locomotive to run in Russia and the first to run in Canada.

Timothy Hackworth is best remembered for his engine *Sanspareil*, which he entered in the Rainhill Locomotive Trials in 1829. In 1840 he resigned from the Stockton and Darlington Railway to concentrate on his Shildon works. There he built what he considered to be his masterpiece, *Sanspareil No. 2*.

Timothy Hackworth improved the efficiency of the steam boiler and introduced the spring safety valve, among many other firsts. He was one of the most skilful and talented of the Industrial Revolution's engineers. He was also a Wesleyan Society preacher. He died on 7 July 1850.

CHAPTER 6

Southern Durham and Teesside

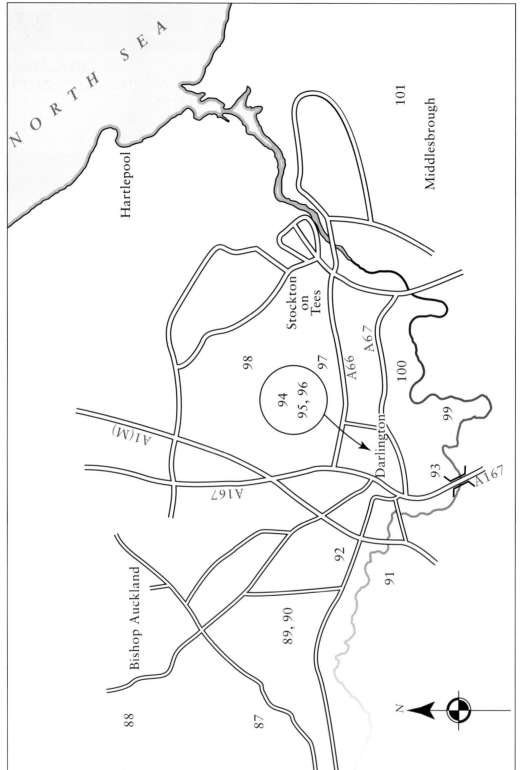

South Durham and Teesside.

RABY CASTLE

¾ mile north of Staindrop

87

OS Grid Ref:
129217

Raby Castle, the family seat of Lord Barnard, is a very impressive fortress set in beautiful parkland where red and fallow deer roam.

Its beginnings were humble: a ninth-century fort, which came into the possession of the Neville family in the twelfth century. Geoffrey Neville, son of Isabella de Neville, was the first lord of Raby, which the Nevilles held until 1569, when they plotted the Rising of the North, a plan to replace Elizabeth I with Mary Queen of Scots. It was a failure, and the Raby Castle estate was forfeited to the Crown. In 1626 Sir Henry Vane purchased Raby Castle, which was stormed for its first and only time during the Civil War by Royalists, the Vanes being Parliamentarians.

Following the restoration of Charles II Henry Vane's son, also called Henry, was beheaded. William III returned Raby Castle to the Vanes and bestowed on them the title 'The Lords Barnard'. A former Lady Barnard, known as the 'old hell cat', haunts Raby Castle. It is said that she is seen on the ramparts at dusk, knitting.

THE CASTLES

88

OS Grid Ref:
103331

1½ miles north-west of Hamsterley

The Castles is probably an ancient British camp, mostly a scattering of stonework in a woodland clearing on the side of a south-facing slope. On three sides is a deep gully, and a small stream has worn a deep, V-shaped valley along the fourth side. The whole site is confined within four walls, over 10ft thick in places. Although no artefacts have been found at this lonely spot, it seems that the arms of a young woman have been found here. Finds like this raise questions. Did she live here? Was she the victim of some awful crime? Why are just these arm bones left here? The questions invite more questions than they bring answers. One thing is certain: this is a remarkable thing to find in a wood. It is an enigma wrapped in a puzzle and, as such, adds interest.

GAINFORD SPA

¾ mile north-west of Gainford, left of the Winston road

89

OS Grid Ref:
162174

Descending from a lay-by on the Gainford to Winston road, a pleasant path will lead you along the tree-lined riverbank to a mineral water fountain, short of a rocky outcrop. This is Gainford Spa. It was established during the late eighteenth century, and as its popularity increased a fountain and a standpipe were installed. News of the health-giving spa water quickly spread and Gainford became a popular retirement place for people in the Darlington area. Gainford itself spread as guest-houses were built around the village green. Plans were made to pipe the water from the Spa itself to the village green, but the project never materialised. The Spa continued in use until the outbreak of the First World War. Then, in more recent years, mindless vandals badly damaged the casing that capped the sulphurous spring water. In 2002 a replacement basin and fitting were installed. So, if you want to give your health a treat, try a small dose of the clear, strong-smelling water.

GAINFORD ACADEMY

90

OS Grid Ref:
174168

In the middle of Gainford

Arthur Stanley Jefferson was born in Ulverston in 1890, but his formative years were spent in the North-East. His father ran a string of theatres and in 1897 the Jefferson family was living at South View, Bishop Auckland, when Stan's parents decided that living so close to a theatrical atmosphere was not best for him, and he was sent as a boarder to Gainford Academy, Gainford.

Those three years at Gainford Academy greatly developed Stan's comic genius. While there, he insisted on entertaining, but it was only through his own lowly opinion of himself that he later developed into a great funny man. He said years later: 'I wasn't fit for anything but comic.' When he was living in America and had changed his name to Laurel and formed a magical partnership with Oliver 'Babe' Hardy, he became the creative member of the peerless, immortal kings of cinema comedy, Laurel and Hardy; and the three years at Gainford Academy played their part.

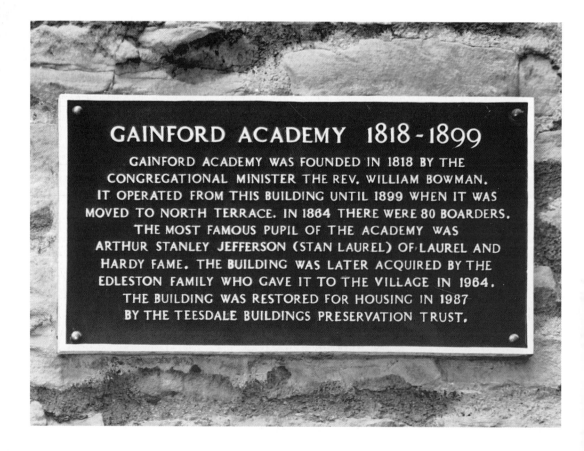

GAINFORD ACADEMY 1818-1899

GAINFORD ACADEMY WAS FOUNDED IN 1818 BY THE CONGREGATIONAL MINISTER THE REV. WILLIAM BOWMAN. IT OPERATED FROM THIS BUILDING UNTIL 1899 WHEN IT WAS MOVED TO NORTH TERRACE. IN 1864 THERE WERE 80 BOARDERS. THE MOST FAMOUS PUPIL OF THE ACADEMY WAS ARTHUR STANLEY JEFFERSON (STAN LAUREL) OF LAUREL AND HARDY FAME. THE BUILDING WAS LATER ACQUIRED BY THE EDLESTON FAMILY WHO GAVE IT TO THE VILLAGE IN 1964. THE BUILDING WAS RESTORED FOR HOUSING IN 1987 BY THE TEESDALE BUILDINGS PRESERVATION TRUST.

91

OS Grid Ref:
212155

PIERCEBRIDGE: GRANDFATHER'S CLOCK

3½ miles west of Darlington

> My Grandfather's clock was too large for the shelf
> So it stood many years on the floor.
> It was taller by half than the old man himself
> But it weighed not a pennyweight more.

It stood in the George Hotel, Piercebridge, for many years and has been celebrated in song. Darlington-based clockmaker James Thompson made it during the early nineteenth century and it featured Christopher Charge, one-time landlord of the George Hotel. Christopher Charge left the George Hotel and when, years later, he returned to live in the George Hotel, he brought his favourite clock back with him. When he became confined to bed his grandfather clock was brought into his room. When his health deteriorated he would point to the clock when it needed winding. Shortly after Christopher's death, the clock stopped and all efforts to restart it failed. Later on Henry Clay Work, an American, heard of the links between the clock and Christopher Charge and wrote the ballad 'My Grandfather's Clock'.

HIGH CONISCLIFFE CHURCH

92

On the south side of Coniscliffe village

OS Grid Ref:
227152

High Coniscliffe church is the only one in England dedicated to Edwin, son of Aella, who was driven into exile by Ethelfrith of Bernicia, returned to kill him in AD 616 and became King of Northumbria and overlord of the southern English. He married Aethelberga, daughter of Ethelbert of Kent, who brought Christianity to Northumbria. Edwin was baptised in 627 and died at the battle of Hatfield Chase.

The church occupies a brilliant site, high above the River Tees on the south side of the village, the original name of which was King-cliffe. The church is long and narrow with a high, spire-topped tower. It has a two-storeyed, crenellated vestry at its eastern end and, at its western end, a golden weathercock. Down the years much building work has taken place in the church, but the Norman door to the north has survived it all. Three cheers for the Normans.

93

OS Grid Ref:
281109

HELL KETTLES

Almost 1 mile north-west of Croft

Hell Kettles is two (once one) closely spaced pools to the south of Darlington. The deeper of the two ponds is 20ft. They are both approximately 30yd in diameter and look ordinary, but the water contained in them has always been sulphurated. They have always been associated with fear and superstition. The pools have been linked with many strange tales, one of the oddest being that of their formation on Christmas Day 1179, told by Abbot Brompton of

Jervaulx Abbey. On that day the ground rose until it was as high as the tops of the surrounding hills. It remained like that all day, before falling, with a tremendous noise, at sunset. Then the ground fell in and swallowed the mound of earth, leaving a deep pool where the mound had stood. Frightened locals thought that the end of the world was close and folklore soon grew around Hell Kettles.

One explanation of their formation is that a dramatic movement of the earth's crust caused a build-up of gases in the magnesium limestone. This is perhaps the most powerful natural phenomenon in County Durham.

94

OS Grid Ref:
289158

LOCOMOTION NO. 1

In the Railway Museum, Darlington

In the summer of 1825 *Locomotion No. 1* arrived at Aycliffe level, carried on a trolley, and a disappointed crowd cried: 'This is the iron horse! Why it's nothing but a steam engine set on wheels!' It was placed on the rails, its boiler was filled with water, and wood and coal were made ready for lighting. But no one had a light and matches were virtually unheard of. George Stephenson prepared to send someone to Aycliffe for a lighted lantern when Robert Metcalfe, a navvy, offered him a burning glass – a convex lamp concentrating the sun's rays at its focus – saying that as he, Metcalfe, always lit his pipe with it perhaps it might fire the engine. Stephenson invited him to try. Using the burning glass and a piece of tarred oakum, Metcalfe fired *Locomotion No. 1*.

Locomotion No. 1 was the first locomotive with wheels coupled by rods. On 27 September 1825 it pulled the first train on the Stockton and Darlington Railway, the world's first public railway, which ran to Stockton where stood the world's first railway ticket office. And it almost never happened.

<table>
<tr><td>

95

OS Grid Ref:
291146

</td></tr>
</table>

STEAD'S STONE

Outside Darlington Library, opposite the Northern Echo

W.T. Stead, outstanding editor of the *Northern Echo* from 1871 to 1880, was born at Embleton near Alnwick, Northumberland, on 15 July 1849. He was only 22 years old when he became editor of the recently established *Northern Echo*, which was destined to become the most influential provincial newspaper in England. He was a dedicated newspaper man, with strong views that frequently came into direct conflict with those of the Quakers who had established this most important daily newspaper. In 1874 he married his childhood sweetheart and they moved to a cottage on Darlington's Hummersknott estate where he kept bees, rabbits, dogs, a goat and a pony. The sound of the pony's hooves regularly shattered the peace of the rows of terraced houses as he rode past in the early mornings or after a late day at his office. He tethered his pony and his dogs to an old cheese press in Crown Street opposite, the *Northern Echo*'s Priestgate headquarters. W.T. Stead died in the *Titanic* disaster on 15 April 1912.

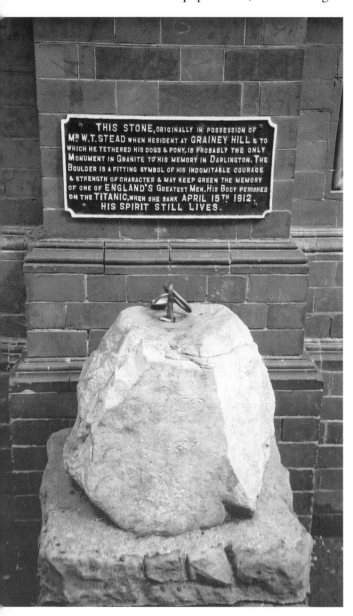

DINO PEPI: DARLINGTON'S NEW HIPPODROME

The junction of Borough Road and Parkgate, Darlington

96

OS Grid Ref:
293144

Dino Pepi was born in 1861 near Florence, Italy. He was an outstanding entertainer, but at the height of his powers gave up performing for a new career in theatre management.

On Monday 2 September 1907 he formally opened the New Hippodrome and Palace of Varieties, Darlington. Heading the bill was Mark Loftus, with a strong supporting cast. In his opening address Dino Pepi said that he was pleased to see so many ladies present because where the ladies were men would follow.

Dino Pepi regularly dressed in an opera cloak and evening dress and was accompanied by his wife and his Pekinese dog.

With the start of the First World War the film industry boomed, and with the advent of wireless, music hall became outdated. Dino Pepi loved horse racing, and some said that he only kept the New Hippodrome because Darlington was convenient for several racecourses.

On 17 November 1927 Dino Pepi died. It was the very day a most memorable performance was being staged at the New Hippodrome. The legendary Pavlova was dancing her 'dying swan'. In a fading spotlight it was both a tribute to Dino Pepi and a warning of the theatrical decay to come.

97

THE COUNTESS OF SADBERGE

2 miles east of Darlington

The name Sadberge is derived from Sac Beorth, meaning 'the court on the hill'. It has always been a place of considerable wealth since it was abandoned as a Roman fort and became the site of the Saxon witenagemote, where prelates and officials would meet to discuss judicial affairs and administrative matters.

Sadberge was a county long before Durham became one. It had its own sheriff, assize court and coroner. Its earldom is still one of the titles attached to the Crown. A prominent grey boulder at the centre of Sadberge village green carries an inscription that reads:

> This stone was placed here to commemorate the jubilee of Queen Victoria, Queen of the United Kingdom, Empress of India and Countess of Sadberge, June 20th, 1887.

It was found 12ft below the surface when Longnewton Reservoir was built. It had become detached from the rock in the west and been deposited by a glacier.

98

OS Grid Ref:
368208

BISHOPTON CASTLE

On the southern outskirts of Bishopton

Before Roger de Conyers built twelfth-century Bishopton Castle the locals called the mound on which it stands Fairy Hill. Many believe that it has survived because of the little people. On one occasion an attempt was made to demolish the mound. As the digging began a voice asked, 'Is all well?'

'Yes,' a workman replied.

'Then keep well when you are well and leave the Fairy Hill alone,' the voice advised. The digging stopped; the mound is still there.

Roger de Conyers built Bishopton Castle to defend his base at Bishopton against the Scots. He built a Norman motte-and-bailey castle, but mainly of wood, not stone. Conyers made good use of the surrounding low-lying land for defence purposes; and in 1143 he was able to resist an attack from rebel forces. Little is known of Bishopton Castle after that.

CONYERS' FALCHION, SOCKBURN

99

OS Grid Ref:
349072

4 miles south-east of Darlington

During the Crusades it is said that Sockburn was surrounded by marsh, where lived an evil-smelling worm or 'fiery flying serpent', which terrorised the area. It fed on pigs, sheep, cattle and humans. Sir John Conyers, Lord of the Manor of Sockburn, vowed to kill the vile creature. Donning full armour, Sir John prayed for help all night in All Saints' Church. At dawn he took the family broadsword, the Conyers' Falchion, and, when the worm turned up, had a desperate fight with it, which he won by chopping off its head. He offered a prayer of thanksgiving and everyone rejoiced.

The worm was buried in a deep hole in a field, and the hole was capped with a huge boulder, which remains there to this day.

The king granted the Manor of Sockburn to the Conyers family for ever, and decreed that the symbol of their ownership, the Conyers' Falchion, should be presented to each new Prince Bishop crossing the River Tees at Sockburn. This ceremony most recently took place on 4 July 2003, when the new Bishop of Durham, Dr Tom Wright, was presented with the falchion by the then dean, the Revd John Dobson.

100

OS Grid Ref:
383113

NEWSHAM MEDIEVAL VILLAGE

2 miles east-south-east of Middleton-One-Row

In the late eleventh century up to twenty-five dwellings formed the medieval village of Newsham. Each had a stone foundation, mud walls and a garden enclosed by mud walls.

During the fourteenth century the villagers gradually moved away. At the same time interest in keeping cattle shrank and sheep farming became the thing to do. The vacated homes were not occupied by other people; sheep were housed in them as sheep farming replaced human habitation. This strange state of affairs continued throughout the fourteenth century until, by the late fifteenth century, Newsham village had only one inhabitant.

A former chapel that now houses the local branch of the Women's Institute and Newsham Hall, part of which dates back to the fifteenth century, are all that remain of Newsham village. Newsham Hall stands at the north-west corner of medieval Newsham, overlooking the remains of the village.

ROSEBERRY TOPPING

1 mile north-east of Great Ayton

101

OS Grid Ref:
579126

Roseberry Topping, on the fringe of the Cleveland Hills, is one of the best-known natural features in Cleveland. It has a distinctive conical shape, created by the collapse of underground iron mine shafts, which has earned it the name 'the Cleveland Matterhorn'.

Once, sailors on the nearby North Sea gauged changing weather conditions from Roseberry Topping as this rhyme, which warns of a thunder storm, indicates:

> When Roseberry Topping wears a cap,
> Let Cleveland then beware of a clap!

When James Cook, probably Cleveland's greatest son, lived at nearby Airy Holme Farm, he would watch ships at sea from the summit of Roseberry Topping; and now, people climbing to its top can see Captain Cook's Monument and, by turning their heads, the Cleveland coast. The two are inseparable.

Roseberry Topping was originally called Odinsburg after Odin, the Norse god, but today's name is much more romantic. Three great walks, the Cleveland Way, the Samaritan Way and the White Rose Walk all meet at Roseberry Topping. It is owned by the National Trust.

The Devil's Door, St Romald's Church, Romaldkirk (see page 20).

FURTHER READING

100 Walks in County Durham, Crowood Press, 1992

Martin Dufferviel, *Durham: 100 Years of History and Legend*, Mainstream Publishing, 1996

Charlie Emett, *Pub Walks in County Durham*, Countryside Books, 1996

——, *Durham Railways*, Sutton Publishing, 1999

——, *Pub Walks in County Durham*, Countryside Books, 2005

——, *Pub Walks in County Durham and Teesside*, Countryside Books, 2006

The County Durham Book, Durham County Council, 1999

Philip Nixon, *Exploring Durham's History*, Breedon Books, 1998

Bill Payne, *Middleton-in-Teesdale and Neighbouring Villages*, Tempus Publishing, 1999

Parkin Raine, *Teesdale in Old Photos*, Alan Sutton Publishing, 1994

Michael Richardson, *Memory Lane: Durham City*, Breedon Book Publishing, 2003

Emma Roberts, *Hidden Places of Northumberland and County Durham*, Batsford, 1994

David Simpson, *Vole of the Vikings*, Smith Settle, 1999

Robert Woodhouse, *County Durham: Strange but True*, Sutton Publishing, 2004

INDEX